Lessons

In

Law of

Attraction

Lessons In
Law of Attraction

Miriam Wartell

Printed in the United States of America
First Edition
ISBN: 978-0-578-65417-1

Why This Book Now?

Currently, we live in a world where so many people worship money, technology and material things more than G-d. Hope has seemingly been lost among many. My goal in writing this book is to be able to help restore the light and love that this world needs. I hope that people will use the power of faith, positivity and Law of Attraction to bring this world back to the spiritual and emotional paradise that it was meant to be.

A note to my readers:

Throughout this book, you will see that I write "G-d". I do this out of respect so this way, if any book is ever discarded or ruined; G-d's name will not be thrown out, recycled or otherwise disrespected. There is a Jewish custom to not write out His Name or any reference to Him explicitly.

Table of Contents

Acknowledgements   I

Preface   V

My Backstory   VII

My Journey   XI

What is Law of Attraction?   1

How Does Law of Attraction Work?   3

TRADITIONAL LAW OF ATTRACTION CONCEPTS

Abundance vs. Lack   5

The Universe is Like a GPS   6

Resistance   8

Vibration and Alignment   8

Allowing   9

Feel It Before It Happens   9

EXPANDED LAW OF ATTRACTION CONCEPTS

G-d Wants to Give Us Good   13

Gratitude   13

Making a Vessel   14

Changing One's Self and Shifting Into a Better   14
Version of You

The Mirror Concept   15

Watch Your Words – Abracadabra   16

Decision Making   16

Write Down What You Want   17

Vision Boards   18

Sending Energy   19

The Inner Controls the Outer   21

Aligning Energies   22

G-d Says YES   25

THE LESSONS I'VE LEARNED

Don't Try So Hard   27

Intuitive Action vs. Negative Impulse   29

When Darkness Clouds Our Light   31

The Three Pillars of Life Change   34

There Is Nothing Other Than G-d   37

Afterword   41

MY JOURNAL   45

POINTS TO REMEMBER   87

A NOTE ABOUT GRATITUDE   89

CONCLUSION   91

Acknowledgements

Life is a journey and the wisdom of others has helped me tremendously. The concepts and stories within this book were the results of the most beautiful seeds of knowledge planted by others. The list of these sources is as follows:

<u>Louise Hay</u> – I read her books *You Can Heal Your Life* and *The Power is Within You*. I would recommend them to anyone looking to understand what self-love is and how affirmations work. Her books taught me just how much life mirrors what we think and feel and gave me much hope for healing.

<u>Payal Aggarwal a.k.a Affirmation Addict</u> – I found her profile on Instagram and began listening to her podcasts. She explains well the "DOs" and "DON'Ts" of affirmations and how to easily manifest the things we desire.

<u>Esther "Abraham" Hicks</u> – I found her videos on YouTube while watching related videos on Law of Attraction. Esther claims to channel her spiritual guides which she collectively refers to as "Abraham" (named after the Abrahamic religions). She channels her guides in a meditative state providing advice to audience members. While her process may be controversial to some, whether or not she is channeling or just giving her own advice, she is rather entertaining and the information she provides I have found to be rather helpful. "Abraham" has taught me quite a lot, but her advice on how to focus on *why* we want things, as opposed to just *what* we want, has been the most helpful and clarifying piece when it comes to manifesting our desires.

I

<u>The Anonymous Author of</u> *The Secret to Miraculous Salvations* – This book was recommended to me by my friend, Meira Joselit. It emphasizes how much G-d loves us and wants to shower us with endless good. It served as a basket to hold all the other knowledge that I've learned and put so many things into context. It's an absolutely wonderful book that I highly recommend. I should note though that some of the words and terminologies are in Hebrew and are not translated as the book is geared towards an audience that understands Hebrew and basic Jewish religious concepts.

<u>Gedale Fenster</u> – Gedale is a successful businessman who overcame addiction and found his path through connecting to a Jewish Chassidic sub-sect, known as Breslov. Gedale lectures all over the world and has numerous videos on YouTube, as well as podcasts. He is one of the few people I have come across who incorporates the topic of Law of Attraction in his Torah-based Jewish lectures.

I would also like to thank:

Dr. Jacquilen Tomas, Ali, ND – Thank you for teaching me and guiding me during this process.

A special person who prefers to remain anonymous – Thank you for bringing so much good into my life.

My Mom – Thank you for being my sounding board, emotional support center and proofreader.

Rhonda Hoffman – Thank you for your help with editing this book.

Meira Joselit – Thank you for your support, advice and endless bounty of helpful resources.

Dena Hundert – Thank you for your guidance, support and the seeds of knowledge that you planted.

Charlene Aminoff – Thank you for teaching me and the rest of the world about Nishmat Kol Chai, a powerful prayer of thanksgiving.

Lastly, I want to thank G-d for providing me with this life-changing information and for allowing me to share this wealth of information with others.

Preface

G-d created the world with His words. He spoke this world into existence. What most people don't realize is that G-d, in essence, gave us the same power. Every word we speak, every thought we think and every emotion we feel creates our reality. This concept, originating from Kabbalah (Jewish mysticism), is what has become commonly known as Law of Attraction.

In talking about this from a general religious perspective, my views of this are as follows: We've all heard of the story of Adam and Eve and the Garden of Eden. It was like heaven on earth. Then, Eve, coerced by dark forces, to say it simply, ate from The Tree of Knowledge. She then convinced Adam to do the same. The Tree of Knowledge brought the knowledge of good and evil. It hadn't been differentiated before.

The concept of Law of Attraction is basically that whatever you focus on expands, meaning, whatever you focus on, you will get more of. Well, what happens when something "new" is introduced to your life? By nature, you focus on it! In other words, it is my belief that it's not that G-d kicked us out of The Garden of Eden, it's that, when we learned about evil, by nature we focused on the negatives and that is how the world got to where it is today. I'm probably not the first person to share this claim or concept, but these are the thoughts that I've had as I've learned this.

This realization came to me from experiencing life's contrast. I told someone that I felt like I went through hell to get to heaven on earth because when I learned what I'm about to share with you, it simply felt like just that — *heaven on earth.*

Since learning about Law of Attraction, good things have come easier to me, there has been a feeling of lighter energy and I finally have explanations for most, if not all, of the hard things I've gone through. My goal is to share my journey and the lessons I've learned with as many people as possible in an effort to make our world the positive place it's supposed to be.

My Backstory

Everything I am writing in this book is based on my personal journal and the things that I have learned over the past year. Maybe at some point I will publish my full journal, but in the meantime, I am publishing the lessons from it and select pages.

I started my main journaling in February of 2019. My journal was meant to be a coping mechanism, my therapy and a safe outlet for my emotional release. I didn't follow any particular type of journaling system. I instead chose a creative approach and did whatever felt right. During February and March, I went through one of the most difficult tests of my life. It was like the largest dark cloud had completely overcome my life or like G-d put His hand to block the road I was on and I had no understanding as to why. During that time, I thought I lost everything. I went through immense emotional pain and embarrassment. I couldn't eat, my body wasn't handling the stress well and overall, I could barely function. I couldn't put time into my commission-based job. I told those close to me that I couldn't even think about work and that "somehow G-d would take care of it." I spent many days crying and screaming and yelling and for the first time ever in my life, I experienced rage.

During that time though, despite my pain, I remembered something I had read in several Jewish books and that was to always say "thank you," no matter what. So I thanked G-d. I had no idea how or why but for one of the first times ever, I listened to the advice of others and implemented it. My ego no longer existed, I honestly had nothing to lose.

It was also during that time that I had started to say a special prayer called Nishmat Kol Chai. Nishmat Kol Chai is a prayer that is typically recited during the Sabbath morning prayer service. I had learned about it in the summer of 2018 from a popular Jewish Instagram account run by Charlene Aminoff who had publicized that when said for 40 consecutive days, creates miracles. I started saying that prayer daily as soon as I heard about it. Immediately, I noticed things got better in my life with regard to interpersonal relationships and great opportunities happening with work. The crazy thing was, months later, during the hardest test of my life, when I didn't even know how I was going to survive each day, I found out that the whole time, I wasn't saying the prayer in full. I misunderstood where it ended and stopped short. Apparently the prayer was several paragraphs longer and I had only been saying the first main paragraph.

You may wonder why it mattered so much, but as someone who has been through a lot, I felt like I needed every miracle I could get it. So there I was, in the midst of my hardest test, starting over with this prayer.

Everything has Divine timing.

In the duration of those 40 days of saying Nishmat Kol Chai in full and ever since then, I have experienced endless miracles. What I thought was the worst thing that I ever experienced turned out to be one of the biggest miracles of my life and set the pathway for everything I'm about to share with you.

The thing is, during that hard time, when I could barely work and all I could do was cry, pray and journal, I somehow managed to make more money than I had ever made in a given month, I learned to soothe myself in ways I never could previously and I managed to find hope. Most importantly though, G-d gave me access to such a gift of knowledge, which largely came through my journaling, in addition to other media.

Nishmat Kol Chai is a prayer of "thanks" and in those first 40 days when I recited it in full, I learned about what is commonly known as "Law of Attraction," but honestly, it was so much more than that. When I put the pen in my hand and the ink touched the paper of my journal, it was like magic happened. My assertive, ego-based self surrendered and the words flowed. What I got was intuition, guidance and help from Above. I received answers to prayers and ways to help myself and others in ways I could not have even imagined.

There are words that I cannot explain and guidance that I cannot take credit for. I learned about a life's journey. Throughout this book, I will be sharing what I learned about Law of Attraction, its Jewish roots and lessons from my journal and other resources.

My Journey

It was a journey of self-love that led me to where I am now. In the summer of 2018, I was frantically searching Google for some much-needed life guidance. I saw an interesting series of blog posts talking about self-love, stating that self-love is the key to everything and it is truly amazing how incredibly accurate that turned out to be.

That July was also my first session with Dr. Jacquilen Tomas Ali, a naturopath who does a holistic therapy known as BodyTalk, a practice that involves asking the body a series of "yes" or "no" questions through muscle testing.

Jacquilen and I first connected through my first full-time job in 2012. I was working for a start-up company at the time that was selling wellness products and services. I had "randomly" found Jacquilen in an online search, learned briefly about the work she does and signed her up to be a vendor. Of all the vendors I signed up, I somehow always remembered her, and clearly, it was for a reason.

In March of 2017, I attended a Small Business Expo related to my job. While at the expo, out of nowhere, I started to feel really ill. My coworker helped me get to a less-crowded side room where I could sit down. Moments after I got there, Jacquilen walked by. I recognized her immediately from her picture – something I rarely do. I jumped up to greet her, introduced myself and asked if she had remembered me. She laughed as she said yes, giving me the warmest hug as if she had known me forever. *In life, there are no coincidences.*

Jacquilen and I stayed in touch since we met. We had periodic calls and she always spent time talking to me and giving me guidance but it wasn't until July of 2018 that I went to see her professionally. In our first session, she told me the exact same thing that Google did, that I needed to work on self-love. At that time, I thought "if anything, I love myself too much," but I later realized that was my ego talking. When I realized that the journey to self-love was much deeper, I e-mailed her saying, "Hi Jacquilen, can you explain to me what self-love is and what needs to be done to 'accomplish' it?" She wrote back saying "Instead of me telling you, you're going to be able to tell me very soon. I'm going to give you an affirming statement that you will say aloud every morning while looking in the mirror. You only need to say it once each morning.

First, it's important that you say it aloud and not read it to yourself. You have to hear it. Second, you must look in the mirror while saying it to know that the message is for you. Say it every day starting tomorrow morning (July 25th) until October 25th." She told me that it takes approximately 90 days to change thoughts and behavioral patterns and to use the affirmations below to retrain my subconscious mind.

I Love Myself Unconditionally.
I Forgive Unconditionally.
I Love Myself Unconditionally.
I Feel Myself Loving Myself Unconditionally.
I Forgive Myself Unconditionally.
Thank You, Thank You!

Within two weeks of saying that affirmation, everything started to change. A big career opportunity opened up for me and my intuition started to guide me in the most wonderful way to the things that I desired most.

The same concept of self-love led me to Louise Hay's books, as well as many of the other resources that I reference in my acknowledgements. Without them, I wouldn't have known how to help myself during my "time of darkness," which in reality, was a time of light. Eventually, the journey led me back to my own roots, the power of positivity and hope, finding love inside of myself and in G-d and the power of saying "Thank You." Throughout my journey, I learned that nothing is impossible with G-d's help.

G-d guides us all to the things that we desire, but to get there, there is self-work. The more we grow and transform ourselves, the more our dreams are within reach. Ultimately though, life is an exploration of ourselves and growing closer to our Creator.

It is with the utmost gratitude that I get to share the tools that helped me and the lessons I've learned.

What is Law of Attraction?

Law of Attraction is the concept that your words, beliefs and feelings create your reality.

Some of us learn habits from our upbringing, but in truth, most of us incarnate into this world to work on certain traits and to grow as people. Our environment just sets the stage for what was always meant to be. Our job is to examine our lives, realize that our experiences mirror our thoughts, feelings and beliefs and to fix them accordingly. Of course, however, there is one vital thing that must be kept in mind throughout this entire process. Whether we feel it or not and whether we realize it or not, G-d created us with love and wants to give us good.

When I started to research the roots of Law of Attraction, I found out that these concepts are based on Jewish Mysticism – what's known as Kabbalah and the Zohar. When I researched other sources from popular bloggers and authors, I noticed that they explain things well but was slightly confused with how some other people reference things. For example, some refer to G-d as "Source" and some as "Universe". Speaking from a Jewish theological perspective, I will say the following: G-d who is the Source of All, created the Universe. He designed the Universe to work in a certain way.

As mentioned in Jewish mysticism, G-d created this world and when He did, He essentially created a vacuum. He created a self-sustaining world where He would remain hidden, yet all that happens would be fair and just through this concept of making our own reality. Of course, we get tested in our lives and as you pay attention to the things that happen in your life and what you go through, you will see that most, if not all, will show a pattern. I initially learned about patterns from Louise Hay, in her book *You Can Heal Your Life.* The background with regard to Jewish mysticism, I learned from a Jewish book titled *The Secret to Miraculous Salvations.* In that book, the author mentions that though G-d restricts Himself, He can be accessed through prayer and contemplation of His boundless mercy and that the fact that He wants to give us good.

The concept behind Law of Attraction is that G-d gave us the power to create incredible, wonderful lives for ourselves. All we have to do is ask, believe and have faith.

How Does Law of Attraction Work?

Law of Attraction is the concept that our thoughts, feelings and beliefs create our reality. By watching our words and mastering our feelings, we can then help change how we feel about ourselves and about our lives and change our reality as a whole.

Affirmations: Affirmations are words you say to help tell your subconscious what you want. Every word that you say regardless of whether it is meant to be an affirmation or not IS an affirmation. With everything that you say, your subconscious mind looks for information and evidence to back up your statements and beliefs and will often create something to happen in your life to reflect that. It is incredibly important to be careful what you say.

Feelings and Energy: Some people refer to a person's energy as their "vibration". The energy and feelings that a person emits can sometimes be even more important and powerful than their words. I can say that I am thankful for something but if while I am saying that I am worried about something, my feeling is focusing on the lack and therefore more lack would come into my life. That's why it's important to feel the positive feelings of what you want to happen as you declare what you want in your life.

Example: Someone affirms "I have a wonderful career and I love that I get to help people and make money while doing it." That affirmation needs to be coupled with the feelings of happiness and excitement in order to be effective. If I say that while feeling worried that where I want to be in my career has not happened yet, I will stay in a place of not having it happen. Our "vibrations" (feelings) create our reality.

When bringing this into a religious perspective, I realized that the feelings that we should all be feeling of happiness, excitement, security, etc., are really just an expression of faith. If we believe that G-d is giving us something good, we feel a positive feeling. We have faith that we either have it or it's coming.

The best way I can explain it is like this: Say you only have $200 in your bank account but you know you're getting a gift of $5,000 that's coming to you in two days. Would you still be worried that you only have $200, or would you be excited and grateful about the $5,000 that you know is coming? **Everything in life that you want to happen can be described by this concept.** Also, if you want money, ask yourself how you would feel if you got x-amount of dollars and then imagine it, feel that feeling and hold onto it. Likewise, if you feel you are undeserving of money or something else good happening to you, unfortunately that can manifest as well.

Think of it this way, **the subconscious always says "YES".** So if you say (via words or beliefs or feelings) "I am attracting lots of money," the subconscious says "yes". If you say "I'm a failure, nothing has or is coming through for me," the subconscious also says "yes".

Note: I keep saying subconscious, however this is really energetic and spiritual law. Law of Attraction is both scientific and spiritual. Think about it, G-d wants us to truly believe in Him. Everything we go through in life is a mirror of what we think and believe. It is important to change our beliefs to help us attract the best possible life.

Payal Aggarwal, also known as "Affirmation Addict" on her social media, does a wonderful job of explaining how affirmations work. From her podcasts and social media content, I learned that every word we say IS an affirmation and that affirmations are so much more than just nice messages we say to ourselves. I highly recommend that you check out her work.

TRADITIONAL LAW OF ATTRACTION CONCEPTS

Abundance vs. Lack

G-d gave us amazing gifts being able to live in the world that He created. What we should give in return is gratitude. We have the power of choice to focus on the positive or the negative. As I mentioned in my opening statement, since the time of Adam and Eve, we seem to be more inclined to the negative. Why? Because it's novel to us. We are eternal beings made in G-d's image. G-d is the epitome of love and mercy. Therefore, we are also made with love and are loving beings. My theory is that when things are novel, our attention goes to it. Because we are eternal, loving beings, evil and negative forces are essentially "new to us," and have been ever since Adam and Eve ate from the Tree of Knowledge. This is why I believe we are naturally attracted to the "lack".

The contrast of Abundance and Lack is a fundamental basic with regard to Law of Attraction. What our attention goes to, we attract. People have a choice to be in one of two modes, that of gratitude in which we give thanks or that of ingratitude in which we complain. Miracles come from gratitude and positivity. People complaining is why the world is the way it is today.

Life isn't perfect, but through perfect perception, we can in essence, make our lives perfect. The goal of Law of Attraction is to state what you want clearly and then align with G-d's energy (some people call G-d "Source"), but you can only do that in a state of gratitude. It is therefore vital to focus on the abundance and not the lack.

As I wrote in the chapter on "How Does Law of Attraction Work?"

the "abundance vs. lack" mindset is the difference between you focusing on something being on its way to you versus the fact that you don't (yet) have it.

The general concept of "abundance vs. lack" is something that I initially learned from Affirmation Addict in that we should always focus on the fact what we want is coming rather than that we don't (yet) have it. I have also learned about this from many others. Virtually every person who teaches about Law of Attraction will focus on this as it is a primary concept.

The Universe is Like a GPS

G-d created the Universe and according to the classic rules of Law of Attraction, the Universe will always bring you what you ask. The thing is, many times, we ask for things both consciously and unconsciously and with our energies, not just our words. We therefore need to be mindful and careful of this.

In learning about this, I relate it to the Jewish concept of G-d creating the world and restricting Himself, but having things be self-sustaining and within a system where things happen in a fair and just way. In my perception, this system that G-d created is what others refer to as the "Universe".

Any Law of Attraction coach or blogger will tell you the same thing — the Universe always says "yes". Whether you have positive thinking or negative thinking, the answer is always "yes". It's kind of like Henry Ford's quote "whether you think you can or think you can't, you're right." Many motivational speakers, business moguls and other successful people all seem to subscribe to the "it's all in your mind" mentality. The thing is, if you decide that you can and will, G-d (via the Universe) will help you.

We attract what we want, but what we want is not just on a human level, it's also on a soul level. Many "Law of Attraction" bloggers and coaches will talk about a person's Higher Self, the part of the soul that stays in Heaven and doesn't come into this world with our body. We can choose to connect to our Higher Selves for guidance but it's our human selves that have free will to make decisions.

When a person declares what they want, the Universal GPS sets its coordinates. When a person thinks about what they like, the Universal GPS sets its coordinates. When a person thinks about what feels good to them, the Universal GPS sets its coordinates. This is also true each time a person thinks about what they don't want or like, as well.

Here's an example: A person says "I found a person who I love and think is a great match for me but he or she lives in their parents' house and that bothers me." If you focus on that, first of all, whatever you focus on, you will get more of and secondly, if your desire to be with someone who lives out of their parents' house is too strong or emphasized (meaning stronger than your stated love and appreciation for this person), then the Universe via "Law of Attraction" says ok, we'll find you someone who fits that criteria.

While I do not consider myself to be a Law of Attraction expert, there does seem to be a lot more weight to the positive than the negative. Meaning, while we get more of what we focus on, the good seems to attract much more easily than the bad.

When I first learned about Law of Attraction, I used to think that every time I had a bad thought I was going to attract something negative and freaked out. Thankfully, it doesn't work that way. It works more from our core belief system. The thing is, our thoughts can eventually become beliefs, which is why we have to be cognizant of them.

So what if a person has gotten him or herself into a bad place? Well, you do the same thing that you would do if you were driving, once you realize you're lost, you reset the GPS to the location in which you want to go. No matter where you are, you can always get yourself in the right direction.

Louise Hay did a wonderful job discussing how our core beliefs affect our lives. I highly recommend her books "You Can Heal Your Life" and "The Power Is Within You."

Resistance

As I stated previously, Law of Attraction can help bring you whatever it is that you desire. There's only one caveat... a little thing called resistance. Resistance is what blocks something from manifesting. Resistance could be a person not feeling worthy, the belief that what you want is impossible or a person not being ready for what he or she desires. A person can generally only manifest their desires when there is no resistance or opposition to what they are asking for. That's not to say that they won't get what they want, but it just may not come through the vehicle of Law of Attraction.

It's important to evaluate your beliefs and feelings to make sure that they match what you desire. For example: A person may say "I'd love to be rich." If that person also thinks "I'm never going to make a lot of money because I don't have the proper education or skills," then guess what? They have a block from getting the money they desire.

Esther "Abraham" Hicks has some interesting YouTube videos discussing resistance and the "path to least resistance" as she calls it.

Vibration and Alignment

Many Law of Attraction experts will use the terms "vibration" and "alignment". Vibration is the energy you emit. All energies have a frequency that can be tuned. The goal is to elevate your vibration and align it with what you want. There are heavy and light energies and also what you choose to focus your energy on or align with. Joy is a light energy whereas despair is probably one of the heaviest energies. At one point when journaling, this all became apparent to me as I started to draw a pyramid of energy. We can lift our energies to a higher vibration. All energies have a gradient. For example, despair, the heaviest energy in my opinion, can be lifted with hope, which I would say has one of the lightest energies. You can also align with concepts like love, money, success, etc., by matching your energetic frequency (vibration) to that which you desire. Example: If you want love, love yourself and emit a strong love for other people. If you want money, give charity for the sake of giving and know good will come back to you.

Allowing

Allowing is exactly what it sounds like. The process of allowing involves getting rid of resistance (like negative beliefs) as well as control. It is important that people allow themselves to feel good even while still facing a seemingly negative situation. It seems like often the fear of disappointment makes people uncomfortable when trying to be positive. Speaking from experience, it almost seems like the fall will be harder if you get your hopes up and then turn out to be wrong.

Law of Attraction is so much more than being just generally positive or hopeful. If you understand that your current situation was created from previous thoughts, feelings and beliefs and that all you are going through is just G-d trying to bring things to your attention, then you can be reassured that positive changes to your thinking and feelings will bring positive results as well. It's not about just "feeling good" and allowing things to happen, but trusting that the work that you've done is leading to your desired good and that when you do your part, G-d (via the Universe) will support that.

Some people try a little, not much happens and then they retreat into old habits. Having faith and allowing is kind of like jumping into a swimming pool; how much fun can you really have if you only stick your toes in?

As best as you can, work on letting go of control, doubt and worry and allow yourself to feel things like joy, happiness and prosperity ahead of time as it makes its way toward you.

Feel It Before It Happens

The other main concept is to feel things before they happen. The mind is a powerful thing. We can visualize things and get ourselves to feel emotions based on things that have not yet happened in reality. Many people use feelings to attract what they want. It helps them to get into the right energy and to allow the good things. It prepares you mentally and emotionally, in a sense.

You can ask yourself questions like "what would it feel like to make more money?" and you may realize that it feels like ease or freedom. This allows you to feel ahead of time that feeling of ease and lack of worry.

If you're looking for a relationship or to improve a relationship, focus on the energy of love. Being in a loving energy means looking at life through a lens of love, loving yourself, loving your environment, loving G-d and loving those around you. Self-love is the most important thing with regard to this because you always need to love yourself before you can properly love anyone else.

If you're looking for success, ask yourself "What do successful people look like? How do they dress? How do they feel and portray themselves? How do they look at themselves and the opportunities around them? This gives you an opportunity to visualize yourself looking and feeling better. You can then focus on the feelings of confidence and knowing your own value. You can also choose to feel the feelings of belonging, strength, power or whatever resonates with you. Just make sure to do this from your soul state – don't fake an ego! It's about learning to feel good on the inside so it comes through on the outside.

When trying this out, you'll likely notice the emotional difference of where you are and where you want to be, but once you become more familiar with how you want to feel, you'll be able to get yourself in the right direction.

The logic behind this is that everything starts from the inside. We often look to other people or situations to make us feel a certain way. How many times have you said, "I would feel so much better if I… (fill in the blank)."

The things I tend to hear the most from people are:

- I would feel less stressed (more at ease) if I made more money.

- I would feel better about myself (love myself more) if I looked prettier or lost weight.

- I would be happier if I was in a relationship (felt loved, felt secure, felt wanted).

- I would be happier if I had a job I enjoyed (felt fulfilled, felt I was of value, felt ease, felt positive about my working environment).

- I would feel better if my marriage was better (felt understood, felt ease, felt happy, felt respected).

Almost everything we want in life is to bring us to a certain feeling. Whether that feeling is satisfaction, love, joy, happiness, ease or anything else, it all starts from the inside. G-d created this world in the most amazing unique way that we have to work on ourselves in order to get what we truly desire. Our challenges will always reflect what we need to work on. When we give ourselves permission to feel certain emotions ahead of time, not only are we having faith that they will happen, but we are actively bringing to our attention whatever was blocking us from feeling that feeling in the first place. Once we get to the point of being able to comfortably feel the emotion of what we want ahead of time, then what we are desiring will then soon come.

EXPANDED LAW OF ATTRACTION CONCEPTS

G-d Wants to Give Us Good

One of the best things about the book *The Secret to Miraculous Salvations* is the author's constant reminder that G-d wants to give us good. The book talks about how people should contemplate, ask for and thank G-d for His abundant mercy. I think sometimes we forget the basics. G-d loves us. He created us with love. He wants to give us good. That being said, we should thank Him and be grateful.

Gratitude

Gratitude is the key to all manifestation. You know how when you give someone a gift and they truly appreciate it, how it makes you want to keep giving them gifts? And you know how when you give someone a gift and they don't say thank you or they just give you a quick, non-heartfelt "thanks," that it makes you not want to give them gifts anymore? Well, when we thank G-d for what we have, He gives us more. To me, trying to manifest and attract things without thanking G-d is essentially a spiritual smack in the face. G-d gave us an amazing gift by creating us and this world, and the system of the Universe helping us — not just to get what we want, but to point out how to work on ourselves.

On that note, we should also thank G-d for when things are bad. Why? Because often, when something isn't going the right way, it's to get our attention to make changes so things *can* go the right way. Thank G-d for the awareness of what you do want and the ability to make positive changes. I find that when I've thanked G-d even without knowing why, I started to see the good in the situation and immediately following, whatever I was going through improved.

Making a Vessel

Something interesting that I initially heard from my friend Dena, and then again through Gedale Fenster is the concept of creating a vessel. G-d wants to give us good, but we need a vessel to contain that goodness. The blessings come from a spiritual stream. In Hebrew, we call it "Shefa". That flow is constantly coming to us, but we need the right vessel to receive it. That vessel could be gratitude, feeling worthy, prayer, the belief that what you want can happen, the belief that G-d wants to give you what you've been asking for or any other myriad of things. It may also be a combination of things.

Changing One's Self and Shifting Into a Better Version of You

On the same concept as creating a vessel, I feel a change cannot happen without an internal shift. If the current version of you was eligible to receive the things which you desire, you would have them because G-d wants to give us good. If we don't have what we desire, it means doing some reflection and making positive changes.

I think sometimes people get discouraged because they cannot figure out a logical pathway to get to what they desire. I think what people fail to realize is that that's the point of faith. I think people sometimes have faith in the wrong way, though. They say "okay, if it's meant to happen, it will happen" or they just try to remain generally optimistic and then get mad at G-d if it doesn't happen. But here's the thing, how can you expect change in your life when you remain stagnant?

Early in my career, I thought at some point I would just get my big break. I had periodically changed my tactics and I figured at some point, something has got to give. I spun my wheels for years unable to understand why I kept coming close to success, but the level of success I desired never came through. It wasn't until I shifted myself by letting go of control and letting go of old, unhelpful beliefs that my intuition guided me to the tactical advice that led to my success. I also realized that I cannot do things myself and have success without G-d's help. Every person has a different journey and while the current version of you may not be able to receive what you desire, another, more improved version of you can. Each positive change allows you to receive more knowledge and blessings, getting you one step closer.

The Mirror Concept

Life is a mirror of our thoughts, feelings and beliefs. Many times our upbringing and the things we see and experience in life shape our beliefs. Our observations and beliefs can determine whether we think certain things in life (like making money or finding love) are easy or hard.

My introduction to this concept was from Louise Hay. She taught the world about the importance of self-love and how to take steps towards it. Her books, *You Can Heal Your Life* and *The Power Is Within You*, were incredibly helpful in my journey. Louise conveys easy-to-understand concepts about how our beliefs, specifically our limiting ones, can greatly affect us. Sometimes our beliefs are conscious and sometimes not. Whatever we experience in life is to get us to *reflect* and facilitate growth.

When it comes to beliefs, it's about taking a look at repeating life patterns and experiences and saying "why does this keep happening?", "how do I feel about what I am dealing with?", "what caused me to have this belief?", "what's the underlying issue beneath it?" and "how can I change this underlying belief for the better?"

Sometimes it's not about specific beliefs like "I'm not worthy of good things" or "I'm not meant to have money," but rather "I need to do everything by myself" or "G-d doesn't care about me." The thing is, whatever we believe and feel mirrors and usually will not stop mirroring until the issue is at least noticed, if not fully resolved or changed. To me, the mirror concept is G-d trying to get our attention. Some beliefs are easier to identify than others and some are easier to change than others, but again, it's about introspection.

Watch Your Words – Abracadabra

My friend Meira and I were talking one day and she asked me if I knew what "Abracadabra" really meant. I had heard previously that it was about speaking things into existence and had heard it more frequently as I listened to lectures from Gedale Fenster. Abracadabra refers to the fact that what we say will be created. (It stems from the Aramaic phrase "Avra Kedabra," which translates to "I will create as I speak.") Well, we speak based on what we feel and feel based on what we believe. As I wrote about earlier, everything we say is an affirmation. I cannot stress enough how important it is to listen to our own language because it's the easiest indicator to how we feel about things. (Not to mention, it creates our reality.)

How many times do people say "it's just one thing after another" when something negative happens? How often have you heard people say "well, I guess it's just not meant to be" or "people don't care about me" or "there's no way I am qualified for that"?

When I started listening to my words, it was a major wake up call. First of all, I realized in business how many times I used the word "hard". I made a conscious effort to stop saying it and eventually, I stopped saying it all together. Almost instantaneously, business got a lot easier. I also made a point to stop saying phrases like "I feel bad" when I feel guilty and I am also very careful about what I say about myself and others.

Decision Making

Decision making is by far, one of the most powerful tools. I used to joke around and say that "G-d gave me the ability to do anything I want but cursed me with indecisiveness." While I do not think that I am cursed, I've definitely had to overcome indecisiveness.

Decisiveness is making a plan and sticking to it. Decisiveness is deciding what you want and not getting caught up on the "how". Decisiveness is saying that you're clear in whatever it is that you want and that you're going for it.

A person should not hope for a specific thing and then make multiple back-up plans. You get what you put your energy on, so if you're more focused on backup plans than on what you desire, you have a much higher likelihood of needing those back-up plans! Don't get me wrong — sometimes backup plans are great, especially when it comes to business, but they should never be your main focus. Always be clear on what you want and focus on that.

Write Down What You Want

I gave advice to my brother and three friends. The advice was to focus on what they want, write it down and then to live their lives as if the thing that they wanted was going to happen within six months.

All of my friends, as well as my brother, had immediate success with regard to what they were looking for. One friend paid off debt, one friend realized what her main emotional block was, one friend found the girl that he wants to spend the rest of his life with and my brother got a much-needed job.

While all of them got something out of thinking about what they want and living like what they want is going to happen, my one friend clearly got the most out of it. Both he and my brother wrote down what they wanted, but my friend made a point to keep his list in view and looked at it every day. On his paper, he put a simple description of what he wanted in a woman and found exactly that. My brother wrote the type of job that he wanted (a highly-specific type of research position) and the general area that he wanted to move to. My brother, unlike my friend, didn't keep what he wrote in his view and I'm wondering if he was a bit too specific or if he is on his way to what he wants. Either way, he immediately landed a teaching position and while it wasn't the exact type of job he wanted, it was in the geographical area that he desired. (I should also note that he did the Nishmat Kol Chai prayer for 40 days as well.)

Many successful people talk about the importance of making a decision and also the importance of writing down goals and desires. I feel like some people are hesitant or they're quick to say things aren't possible and they don't try. There's often a fear of disappointment. The thing is, once you establish your desire, you don't have to know how it's going to happen, just know that it will. The thing is once you put your true desire out there, if you're able to do so without the emotional blocks of thinking that for whatever reason it can't happen, then you'll see how G-d will help you.

Vision Boards

Vision boards are essentially collages of all the things that you want in life. You'll see people who have boards with fancy cars and nice homes or sometimes just positive affirmations. Personally, I never thought much of them other than that they were cute and fun but I didn't put much stock into them.

I made my first vision board after listening to a podcast from Payal, aka Affirmation Addict. Her explanation of them seemed a little less fantasy world and a lot more playful and helpful as far as a manifesting tool. I decided to create a vision board, but for the pure purpose of having fun. I decided to create one with the funniest thing I could think of at that time. I made a vision board with the Philadelphia Eagles and, in the center, I put in a picture of my homemade cake and put an affirmation about bringing cake to my favorite player on the team. (I also wrote other affirmations about personal goals as well.) Sure enough, within a very short amount of time (about six months), I was able to bring homemade cake to the exact person I had hoped. It was the funniest, best form of validation.

As far as the other things that I wrote on my vision board, they are in the process of happening (with G-d's help). This is not to say that people should go and make vision boards and assume that a power comes from them. In my opinion, that would be akin to idol worship. The idea is to use it as a tool for a fun way to have faith.

It seems that the real "power" of the vision board is the idea of decision making. It helps people to decide what they want in life. Decision making is one of the most powerful manifesting tools because that sets our intended destination. I strongly feel that G-d supports us in whatever decisions we make so that's all the more reason to make sure that our decisions are positive ones. That being said, never be afraid to make a decision because we always have the power to change our mind.

Sending Energy

Every thought we think and every emotion we feel transmits energy. How we think about ourselves and our lives affects our energy and how we think about others affects their energy.

When I read the book *The Secret to Miraculous Salvations*, there was a story in there about how a woman went to her Rabbi for advice on marital issues because her husband had been lazy and unhelpful. The Rabbi asked her if there was ever a time where her husband was helpful and she could only ever think of one time. The Rabbi told her to think of her husband the way he was during the one instance when he was helpful. Sure enough, he began to be a better husband.

I thought that concept was really interesting and I adapted my own versions of it in my life. There was a point within the last year where a close friend of mine was in the hospital. She could have been in there for weeks, but every day I visualized her as the healthy person I know her to be. Thankfully, she was released from the hospital within the week. I'm not claiming that she was able to heal more quickly solely because of me, but sending positive energy likely helped her.

It's funny because when ants transmit signals, we accept it as nature, but when humans claim to do it, we think it's odd. The thing is, when we think about others, they can't hear our thoughts, but they will get a subconscious pulse of whatever feelings and energy are behind the thoughts that we think about them.

Here's an example: You could be standing in line at the checkout counter and the cashier is being rude and unhelpful to the person in front of you. If you start to think to yourself "I bet this person is actually a really nice person but they're just having a bad day," the odds are that when it's your turn to checkout, the cashier will be more helpful and friendly towards you.

Here's another example: There's someone that you really can't stand and in your mind you're thinking "get away from me." That person will feel that pulse of energy, but the likelihood is that they will actually come towards you because they know you don't want that. If you're indeed having an issue with someone, consider thinking the words "I wish you well, but from far away." This helps create a positive form of distance.

Sending energy can become a big issue when you assume the performance of someone, especially when it is in negative ways. If you think of someone as a "screw-up" or "failure," you're sending out that energy. They are receiving it subconsciously and the likelihood is that, unless they are super-strong emotionally, that's going to make them continue to fail or fail even further. Where this can be easily applied to is sports teams – there is a stadium of people (plus a lot of people yelling at their TVs) sending all kinds of thoughts and energy. If you want your team to win, you need to send them that "I believe in you" energy. The same concept can also be applied to how parents think about their kids and how teachers think about their students.

Imagine the people we can heal – those suffering with both physical and emotional illnesses. When you see individuals struggling emotionally, rather than think how sorry you feel for them, think something like "I bet they are really sweet and fun. I'm sure they are capable of being strong and happy and able to showcase their best traits." If those you care about are going through things, remember a time when they were in a better place emotionally and think of them as that version of themselves. For people dealing with physical issues, think of them when they were in better health and picture them again in that place now.

The same concept applies to thinking about yourself. Many people self-identify with whatever problems or issues they are facing. Remember how you were when you were at your best and know that you have the capability to get back to it.

The Inner Controls the Outer

The entire point of attraction starts within yourself. We are living in a world where we are literally being taught to look at others. We look at others in comparison to see what we "should" be doing as well as for advice. All of the answers we need are inside of ourselves and the experiences we desire we have the power (with G-d's help) to create. So why look to anyone else?

If something happening in your life upsets you, know that you can change it. While sometimes there is indeed a tactical approach and reason to change your outside, the true change always starts on the inside.

If you're having an issue with another person for example, you may need to change your perspective, approach, the way you think about them, the way you think about the situation, your assertiveness or any other myriad of things. However, when you realize that your thoughts and feelings are creating the circumstance to begin with, you can then start to shift your reality and relationships from changes within.

There was a point in my life not long ago where I found myself dealing with unhelpful behavior from someone I interact with regularly. I kept getting upset at the person and the situation and was getting in bad moods as a result. I told myself, I know I should be working on myself and not putting my energy on someone else but… (and then I inserted whatever reasons why I was upset at that person). Since what we think about expands, that obviously didn't help.

When I managed to finally take myself out of the issue mentally and focus on giving myself the same advice I give others, things got better. I focused on strengthening my sense of self, being in the present moment and knowing that G-d is in every situation. I reminded myself that when I get my core energy right, my outer world has to cooperate with that fixed energy. I took a leap of faith, ignored what bothered me, got myself back to where I needed to be emotionally and sure enough, within a matter of days, the entire issue started to subside and change for the better.

Aligning Energies

There is a concept that you can match your energy to what you desire. This is done through emotional and spiritual alignment. Personally, in learning to connect, I always felt that connecting to G-d was more of a vertical energy (where I could, in essence, line up with His light) and the things I desired, whatever subject matter it was, always felt more horizontal.

The most powerful alignment there is, is the alignment with G-d. I like to think of this as a row of vertical lines. In the center of all the vertical energetic lines is G-d's Energy. He is in all of the lines, but the middle line is where you feel His energy the most. The reason I say it like that is to help you visualize alignment. You can visualize yourself lining up with that line. Perfect alignment means perfect faith and perfect openness. From my experience, you can only get there with humility and an open heart. When you align yourself with G-d's loving energy, there's no greater feeling. It feels like pure love and joy and appreciation.

It is a rare but amazing experience to be in that state, and for that reason, we are given healthy curve balls to throw us off. The goal is to continuously get back into alignment. If we were constantly allowed to be in that state of alignment, I don't think it could be appreciated in the same manner.

Then, there is what I consider to be the horizontal energetic lines. The horizontal lines are the situations and things we desire. These are things like money, certain levels of success, qualities of relationships, being in certain places, meeting certain people, etc.

I consider horizontal energies to be things that are in or out of reach. If something is seemingly "in reach," you are very close to being aligned with it. If you have it, you are aligned with. And if you feel it's out of reach, then you most certainly aren't aligned with it, BUT, you can always learn how to be.

Have you ever put a certain person or position on a pedestal? Celebrities are the most classic example. People put celebrities on pedestals and are then often scared to approach them as a result. People feel that they will never get a chance to interact with them because to many, celebrities (or people of high stature) seem to be "above" where the average person is at and therefore, out of reach.

The same is sometimes true with how we feel about anyone in the top of their game whether it is pro-athletes, well-known business moguls or simply your superior at work. How many times does a certain career position seem impossible to attain? It seems impossible, because we are not aligned with it.

So, how do we align with it? Self-work.

I believe Law of Attraction was designed for personal growth. It's not supposed to be the "smoke and mirrors" just feeling good and it will happen approach. It's about knowing what you want in life and knowing that you need G-d to get you there. Things like self-concept, self-worth and self-love all play a role in attaining what you desire but for each person, the journey is different. The one thing I will say, though, is that nothing is impossible.

I'm saying this as someone who has had the amazing experience of extreme faith and also knowing that any other person can experience that, too. When I reference extreme faith, I am referring to times when I was able to align with G-d's energy even when life seemed incredibly dark and seemingly hopeless. Finding that inner light, having faith and feeling that joy ahead of time will forever be one of the most amazing experiences of my life. Even when things have gone well and I've aligned with G-d through gratitude, nothing compared to finding the light in darkness.

When I talk about being on the same level as others, I am referring to knowing that in a sense, we are all equal. No person is ever out of reach. While there are people I admire, respect and appreciate, I do not put them on a pedestal because it doesn't serve me to do so. A person should not do that and especially should never do the opposite and put someone down. The only people that I believe should be held on an elevated level are righteous people who are true in their merits. Still then, it is important to realize that people are people and G-d is G-d.

When I say that no one is out of reach, I say that with real-life experience. I've had the pleasure of meeting a number of famous people, including a former vice president of the United States, a previous governor, a current governor, a current mayor, famous athletes, singers, business leaders and other celebrities. When you approach someone with a calm, inner confidence of knowing you are also of value, the eager, nervous energy doesn't scare them off. Instead, through self-growth, comes a feeling of "I belong" and that's a feeling that I hope that everyone gets to feel.

The big thing in life is to not make a big deal about it (even if you feel it is) because anytime you make a big deal out of something, you are essentially saying it feels out of reach. I cannot stress that point enough. This concept applies to people, jobs, success-levels, money, etc. The goal is to be as comfortable with things as possible.

Never chase anything. Just know that good is coming and enjoy the feeling of knowing that it is.

G-d Says YES

The thing I've come to realize is that almost all the time, if not all the time, G-d says yes. Sometimes He says "not now" which is the same thing as "yes, but later." There was a certain point where I was able to shift my focus and realize that all of the things I have been praying for, G-d has been trying to give me for years, but I didn't have the right vessel to receive it.

(That's also why it's important to meditate or do something to calm our minds so we can get intuitive information to help us.)

The thing is, if we're really not meant to have something, then it's not that G-d doesn't give it to us, it's that we will for some reason be in a state of us not allowing it for ourselves. There may be issues which create emotional blocks for ourselves or issues that create the "not now" or the seemingly "no" but the light is always coming from above, the goodness is always coming from above, it's just a matter of what we want and what we can receive based on our emotional and spiritual state. This is why it's so important to shift into a version of ourselves that is ready for what we desire.

If we are not emotionally ready for things, then how can the good things that we want come to us? We are often either in disbelief or cannot accept what we desire. We often find ourselves feeling unworthy or feeling like there's a catch. Keep in mind, our subconscious minds look for evidence to support what we believe so it's incredibly important to be conscious of our beliefs but it's also incredibly empowering that our beliefs can be changed.

Often there's just some work that has to be done in order to get the goodness we desire. G-d wants to give us good. It's His nature to give us good and if for any reason we are not receiving the good, that's when we need to look inside of ourselves to see where the block is.

This ties into the concept of creating an emotional and spiritual vessel for the things that we have been asking for. We change to become the vessel.

This is also where Law of Attraction comes into play. When we focus on the feeling ahead of time, we in essence get to practice what we want coming to us because we allow ourselves to feel it before it actually happens. It then creates a certain comfort and acceptance of receiving the blessing.

Law of Attraction teaches people to state what they want and focus on the fact that it is coming (a.k.a. faith). It allows us to psychologically, emotionally and spiritually accept it because we essentially experience it happening before what we want takes place. We practice on a soul level, not just an ego level. This practice of knowing our prayers have been answered and feeling positive emotions ahead of time is what creates the vessels for our prayers to be answered. In other words, it's been there spiritually all along, but we practice it so we can accept it until it finally becomes our reality.

THE LESSONS I'VE LEARNED

In less than one year of journaling, my whole life has changed. My entire perspective has changed. There is something so special about self-reflection. The lessons I've learned came from a mix of listening to videos, reading books, journaling and praying.

Don't Try So Hard

One of the biggest lessons I've learned is to not try so hard. The more relaxed and at ease I am about something, the easier it comes. The more I stress, the less easy it comes. It's that push-pull of faith and worry. When people feel the need to try hard, it means there is an underlying belief that something can't happen or that it's difficult. That's why people expend so much energy. Trying too hard is like admitting that you don't have faith or that you're choosing to rely on yourself instead G-d. (That's a major concept in of itself.)

There was something funny that had come to me while journaling. I had taken a moment to check Instagram and I saw a picture of a woman dressed in a way that seemed to be calling attention. (That's my polite way of saying she wasn't wearing much.) She wasn't overtly trying to show off as some women do, but it definitely had an energy of "hopefully someone will see this and think that I'm cute." While we all have our moments, it really made me think about people's constant need for validation, including my own. Here there was this beautiful woman essentially trying to get attention and attract a guy and I couldn't help but think that if she were just herself, she would attract not just any guy, but a guy that's good for her, someone attracted to her soul.

We always get what we attract, so needy energy is a major problem. Trying too hard is like telling the Universe that you are needy and desperate. I am guilty of doing this quite a bit with other things and it was only from journaling that I realized how both funny and ridiculous I was being.

Both in work and my personal life, I can tell you that if I approach someone from a place of trying too hard versus feeling at ease, I will get drastically different results. There are times I have acted in both ways with the exact same people and they will always respond to my energy based on what I put out to them. It doesn't matter whether it's masked or not, people feel energy so it's not about a person's words or actions but the energy that's behind it.

With regard to my work, there have been times where I met with clients and got overly concerned with what they thought of me or what I was presenting to them. I ended up reiterating certain selling points over and over again and it didn't matter how perfect the plan was for them, the clients would often end up saying no or "not now." It took me a while to realize how much my worries had affected my energy. No matter what I did or said, that energy translated. The good news is I eventually realized that if I trust in myself and my abilities then I don't have to think about what the client thinks. I am secure in knowing what I'm doing and can focus on the joy of helping them.

In the more personal realm, there have been many times where I made a lot of mistakes by trying too hard to fix the initial issue. Meaning, there were times where I did something that I should not have done, like said something stupid and then tried to "fix it" by over apologizing (and drawing more attention to it). That was usually followed by worrying about what the person thinks and then texting them a funny or cute picture to see if they respond in a forgiving manner or if I successfully diverted their attention from whatever I did to upset them. It obviously only made things worse.

If I wasn't in a place of worry and was able to use logic, I would have just apologized once and let it roll off my back. However, when worry kicks in, people do stupid things. The thing is, when we try too hard to fix our mess, it just draws more attention to it.

This same concept has been an energetic and emotional struggle for me when it comes to dealing with tougher days. There were times where I would hit rough spots and times of depression and I would do everything I could to make myself feel better, not because I loved myself but because I felt bad about feeling bad. There would be days where I would cry and pray and journal but only feel worse because I would put out such frantic energy of "why am I in this state and why won't it go away?" It took me a long time to realize that the reason the things that used to help didn't help me was because I tried too hard and the reason I tried too hard was because I was hard on myself.

Even after I became aware of it, it still took me some time to accept that I have bad days and to love myself on those days instead of trying hard to push it away. When the day came that I finally looked in the mirror and accepted myself, I was able to stop worrying about *when* the negative feelings would go away and was able to focus on the fact that at some point, the negative feelings *will* go away. The change in focus is now how I get myself out of a funk. The more I tried to force myself to feel better, the more miserable I remained. When I had faith and let G-d control the timing and surrendered to the issue, I felt better almost instantaneously.

Intuitive Action vs. Negative Impulse

Every person takes action in one of two ways, intuition or impulse. They either follow their own inner guidance system or they just react in the moment. I learned a tremendous lesson on allowing my intuition to guide me to take inspired action instead of my fear and impatience having me act on impulse. Acting with guidance has always led me to great things. Impulse led to the opposite.

I realized at a certain point that when I am in a true state of calm, I can actually hear my intuition. For someone who has never noticeably experienced this, this probably sounds rather odd. Everyone has an inner voice. Our decisions are based on logic and what feels good and right to us, but it is our intuition that is our internal GPS. Some people hear their intuition and others feel it. However it comes, true intuition will only come from a positive place. Sometimes intuition can also contradict logic and that's where faith comes in.

All of life's decisions can be felt out. Some of us are more connected to our internal GPS than others. The more we familiarize ourselves with our intuition, the more we can decipher what is intuition and what is impulse, also known as the evil inclination.

It was during my period of perceived darkness that I actually learned to be humble and open enough to clearly hear the inner voice inside of me. I could hear my inner voice guiding me and telling me what I should do. I felt naturally drawn to books that I should read or videos I needed to watch. Each contained answers to information related to questions I had been asking G-d. The way I see it, intuition is our connection to our Higher Selves, the part of us that is always connected with G-d; therefore, when we connect with ourselves, we can also connect to G-d and His answers.

I also learned to understand my body's signals to me. For example, if I was about to make a call or send an e-mail and my muscles tightened or if there was a change in body language, I realized that was my cue to wait. If I was meant to check my phone at a certain time, something non-forced would lead me to it or I would feel this natural, non-impulsive feeling drawing me to it.

Impulsiveness, on the other hand is what leads to the emotional badlands. It is comprised of fear, anger and impatience. Impulsiveness is what trips us up and is the sneaky way that our evil inclination gets us. Impulsiveness says "you must take action now, forget about waiting to feel better, act on your current feelings of frustration, anger or ego." It also says "why wait when you can have instant gratification now?" Everyone has a positive and negative inclination — *like an angel and devil on your shoulder* — and it's up to us to decide which voice and feelings to listen to.

When I was in a place of emotional wilderness, I wasn't looking to take action. I was in a place of being so down that I was just trying to gain some sense of understanding and direction. Because I wasn't looking to take action, having that experience of being naturally guided showed me just how often I was being impulsive. So many times, I've done things out of fear. I realized many times that when we take quick action, it's also an action of "I know best," rather than "G-d knows best," meaning it is fear instead of faith.

Nowadays, I feel many people are disconnected spiritually and emotionally so they may not know how to connect to a Higher Power and feel Guiding Light. The thing is, the Guiding Light is always there; it's just a question of whether we are receptive to it or not. It often takes a lot of self-work and especially a lot of humbling to get to the point of being in the receptive mode. It's kind of like the old TVs that used to have to be on a certain channel to connect to the cable or VCR. The capability is always there but you need to get yourself to the right station.

During the dark time which ended up being the foundation and catalyst of this book, I had no choice but to let go of my ego and be humbled. G-d, in turn, gave me an immense amount of light. For months, once I learned to trust my intuition, my whole life changed for the better. I had an almost unbelievable amount of success with many things in my life and then, of course, while writing this particular chapter, I was tested.

When Darkness Clouds Our Light

It seems just when I had the intention to write the previous chapter, I was tested. I literally typed the headline and then shut down for a couple of weeks. I had never experienced anything like it before. I had become so in-tune with my intuition, but at a certain point, the fear I had made it seem like I slipped on an emotional banana peel. *I never saw it coming.*

It seemed like right when everything was aligning, things turned upside down again – not as bad as it did months before, but a similar type of feeling. The thing is, in one way, this time was better and in one way, this time was worse.

This time was better in the sense that I immediately realized I was being tested. I literally looked up and spoke to G-d letting Him know that I acknowledged this was a test and that I got the message loud and clear: "DO NOT TRY AND CONTROL THINGS." I thought that because I realized the test right away that life would fix itself immediately – nope. Apparently, there was more to it. And, the reason I say that it was in a sense worse than what happened months before was because for the first time ever in my life, I felt like I couldn't connect to G-d's Light and that's obviously a terrible feeling.

Even in my worst times, I always felt a little bit of light, but in this case, for whatever reason, it was like all reception was lost. I was upset, confused and angry. Literally, within the course of a few days, I went from living the most awesome, cool, wonderful life to literally falling on the floor with grief. When the incident that caused this happened, as I said, I knew right away it was a test. I figured if I acknowledged it, it would go away quickly. Wrong. I thought maybe it had to do something with "Mercury Retrograde" (a time where Mercury appears to move backwards and astrologically is supposedly said to cause things to be backwards in peoples' lives) — nope. Even after the retrograde, the issue persisted.

I was truly in a place of emotional darkness. No matter what I did, I couldn't pull myself out of it. I had just learned what I thought was every single thing I (or anyone else) needed in life. I had amazing knowledge and spiritual help written in my journals. I had the wisdom of the videos I watched and the books that I read. I had the power of knowing that G-d can do anything and all I had to do was feel good and align with His positive energy, yet, no matter what, I couldn't get myself to feel good. I just felt lost.

I had prayed to overcome my need for impulsive action, my need for control, my need for instant gratification of knowing things are okay. I cried multiple times because I knew that if I could just get myself to surrender that my intuition would give me the right timing and words if I let it. I wanted to surrender. I wanted to truly feel in my heart that G-d's plan is better than mine. I wanted to feel that sense of self-improvement of having the patience to wait and see that things will be okay. I just couldn't get myself there.

Literally, for several days I prayed for help to overcome my nature. At a certain point, I realized that as much as I wanted to, I couldn't overcome it. It was only at that realization, that I learned something incredibly powerful.

Since I knew I could not overcome my feelings, I asked G-d to help me as I took "impulsive action". I confessed to G-d that as much as I wanted to, I couldn't do better in that state so I said something like "I've tried so hard to overcome my nature and I can't. I know I should wait for my intuition to help me, but I don't feel I can wait. Since I am going to take action, please G-d, help me to take the best action I can take. Please help me to find the best words that I can and please help me with the situation because I cannot do it without Your help."

It was then that what I needed flowed to me. It was just as powerful, if not more powerful, than if I had surrendered and used my intuition the natural way. I had learned a while ago that G-d determines whether we are successful or not. In that particular instance, I was destined to not have success in letting go and surrendering so I could really see G-d's work in another way.

It happens to be that when G-d helped me to find the words for the "impulsive action" of needing to message someone about something I had been holding in, it led me to the exact thing I was hoping for. It led to an open, healing dialog and a huge emotional weight had been lifted.

I realized and learned so much from this test. I had heard so many times that in life it is our job to just do the best that we can. In this case, it was so helpful and validating to know that it's okay to not be perfect all the time. I thought I had all the answers I needed and

G-d showed me that I didn't. I thought I had to be positive all the time and I couldn't. All I had to do was come close to G-d, humble myself and confess, saying, "Please help me, because I cannot do this without You."

The Three Pillars of Life Change

I experienced a massive test before writing this book and another strong test while writing it. In the previous two chapters, I wrote about how G-d answered me when I called out saying that I cannot do things without Him. The thing is, what preceded that was many tearful prayers as well as gratitude.

Three days prior to receiving salvation from the test, I focused on gratitude. I found one small thing to focus on and be thankful for. I felt almost no spiritual light but continued to thank G-d for the test and what I had learned. Each day, I was able to feel the gratitude a little more and then say "Thank You" a little more sincerely. I slowly started to feel the light again.

During those days when I kept saying "Thank You," I noticed a particularly interesting sign. Almost wherever I was, and even on social media, I kept seeing images of keys. Specifically, it was the really old three-prong keys.

When I say that I saw images of keys, I don't mean in my imagination or in a visualization, I mean I literally saw them. For example: I saw images of keys all over various Instagram posts, I noticed my cashier at the store was wearing a necklace shaped like a key, and even at home; the washcloth that was by my sink happened to be one of a certain brand that has an old-fashioned key on the tag. The only reason I had noticed it was because somehow the washcloth had awkwardly turned upside down, showing the tag and my intuitive attention was drawn to it. As simple as it was, I know when something random repeats, there's usually a message attached to it.

I went to Google and searched for a meaning. The top answer was that a key symbolizes the opening and closing of spiritual doors. For me, I realized it symbolized that I had found "key information" that I had been needing.

The piece of information that came to me through prayer was that I shouldn't just look at G-d as the Creator of the problem (test), but should realize that He is the Creator of the solution.

Once I focused on this, everything started to shift and I started to feel light again. That's what led me to the words, "I cannot do this without You" and my salvation from the test.

As much as I write about Law of Attraction, I am reminded that nothing, not even being in a positive mindset can be done without connecting to G-d in some way.

I realized that there are three pillars that can change one's life, they are:

1. **Belief in G-d** (The realization that G-d can do anything. G-d is in every situation. G-d IS every situation. There is nothing other than G-d and G-d wants to give us good.)

2. **Choosing to feel good and align with positive energy** (Find the feeling before it happens, have faith that the good is coming and allow yourself to feel it ahead of time.)

3. **Changing beliefs that no longer serve us** (Everyone has beliefs and old wounds that they need to heal, some conscious and some subconscious.)

When I went through the test while writing this book, I realized several things: I realized G-d was showing me that I need to give up control; I realized G-d wanted me to see that He has the solution; I realized the power of gratitude (because that's what brought the light back); I realized the power of confession and asking for help. I also realized that G-d was helping remind me of the third thing listed which is what made me fearful and step on the "emotional banana peel" in the first place. He finally allowed my core, scary belief to surface and once it did, I started to heal it. I wrote about it in my journal and said "I choose to acknowledge and safely release the fear of...."

Somehow in all the work that I had done, I had gotten so caught up in the inner workings of Law of Attraction, that I forgot one of the basics.

When I talk about life being a mirror, every challenge we have is to get us closer to ourselves and to G-d. The more we come close to ourselves (self-love), the more we can connect to G-d.

As I mentioned in the chapter "The Mirror Concept," Louise Hay's books taught me invaluable information about how our core beliefs will mirror in our reality. The fact of the matter is, a lot of the issues I was experiencing and a lot of the fear and heartache was tied to a painful inner belief about what I *thought* G-d wanted for my life. One of the most recent things I had journaled before writing this was "what if G-d's will is different than mine?" But then I realized G-d's will is for me to be happy and feel good so how could His will be different than mine? They are one in the same. Meaning, if something brings me true joy and happiness, there has to be a reason for that. It must somehow be Divinely led.

Any time something unfortunate or unpleasant happens, it's just a reminder to get to our core selves. When our body has pain, it's there to tell us there's a problem. The same is true spiritually.

Here I was going in circles – for years really – and in reality, all G-d was trying to do was bring the issue up over and over again so I could see the common theme and heal it. It's not always easy to figure out what we need to heal or feel, but it's a first step to look for it. That's why gratitude is so important because even troublesome issues are a gift. They are there to help us make corrections.

G-d only gives us good and it's not necessarily the trouble itself that's "good," it's that it leads to our ultimate healing and rectification and that's *good*.

There Is Nothing Other Than G-d

In Hebrew, there is a phrase and concept known as "Ein Ode Milvado," which means, there is nothing other than G-d. To me, there is nothing more powerful in the world than this concept.

This is the concept that anything can change at any moment and that salvation can come in the blink of an eye with G-d's help.

It is the concept that, in my opinion, not only explains all energetic matters but also "Law of Attraction."

Ein Ode Milvado is the concept that G-d is in everything and everyone. When we send someone energy, when we feel certain energy, when we go through any circumstance – nothing is without G-d. There are many Jewish books on this concept and it has singlehandedly been the most helpful concept in my spiritual learning.

A lot of people believe in the concept of destiny. I personally believe in destinations, but the pathways are up to us. Anything that is destined to happen can also be changed. Sometimes our destiny can be changed by our decisions, but in some cases, can only be changed through G-d. This is the power of Ein Ode Milvado.

I've shared a lot in this book, but what I didn't share is what caused the emotional darkness that led to the light of this book. While I do not feel personally comfortable sharing all the details of what happened, what I will share is the relevant information that led me to this.

I was already familiar with the concept that there is nothing other than G-d. I had heard stories of people struggling with fertility focusing on this concept and then being able to conceive. I've heard stories of people with illnesses having a full recovery. Ein Ode Milvado is the belief in G-d and His miracles, the belief that even against all odds, He can do anything.

One thing I have personally struggled with is the concept of free will and fate. I used to get so caught up in my fears of "what if what I want isn't meant to happen?" Every time I allowed that worry into my vibration (energy), it led to an emotional down-spiral.

I think that is something that everyone can relate to on a certain level. We are scared that what we want isn't possible or isn't G-d's will.

I'm going to tell you right now that if you've ever gone to a psychic, mystic or any figure of the sort, *disregard what they have told you*.

If you have ever gone to a doctor who told you that you have a condition that is permanent or that you are destined to live your life a certain way, *remember that they are not G-d*.

If you have parents, friends or anyone else in your life who told you that you couldn't pursue your dreams, wouldn't amount to anything or told you that you had to live your life a certain way, *do not let your future be defined by that*.

If you've ever had bad thoughts or negative emotions about yourself, *disregard that, too*.

I have fought so much fear, so much pressure and so much influence. I knew no psychic was perfect, but I still feared what was predicted. I knew no doctor was G-d, but still feared I couldn't heal. I knew the people in my community and inner circle all spoke from their own points of reference (and didn't know my situation) but still feared the picture that they painted because it wasn't the picture that I wanted for myself. From different people and different situations, I was told my life had to be a certain way and at one point, all I could do was look up to G-d.

I never went to psychics to know my future. I went and sought advice from a few intuitive and gifted people over the years, but only about general life guidance. The advice I sought was strictly for purposes of physical and emotional healing, but never for fortune-telling.

Any helpful person that is truly intuitive and gifted will not tell your future. Instead, he or she will guide you on how to help yourself. There was only one time when my future was explicitly told to me and it was one of the most horrifying experiences of my life. I was trying to get a phone number for a certain person and someone that I know recommended that I call a particular person to get the phone number. When I called the person to get the phone number, I had no idea ahead of time that she claimed to be "gifted". As an intuitive person myself, I never had an issue with fellow intuitive people. I feel that G-d gives people certain information but all information is open to interpretation and are never absolute truths. That being said, I am intuitive, not psychic.

When I called this woman to get the phone number, she mentioned her ability of knowing things. I had sarcastically asked about my future, not thinking much of it and it ended up being the biggest regret of my life. She was relentless in telling me that I couldn't and wouldn't have what I wanted more than anything in life. She tried to then paint some other pretty picture of what my life would be, but it's not what I had asked for. I had never in my life felt as sorrowful as that day.

In retrospect, I should have never asked about my future, not even in a joking way. G-d made it very clear to me that I am to believe in Him and only Him.

For months, I battled worries. Just a few weeks after that call, I watched my life crumble before my eyes. I had one of my worst fears happen and I thought I lost everything. I couldn't understand how things seemed fine and then suddenly weren't. As tough as the time was, I tried to accept it as G-d's will. I thanked G-d even though I was distraught. I thanked G-d even though I was angry. I thanked G-d even though I was at a point of having to rebuild my life.

It was during that dark time that I received the information that became this book and everything that I thought I lost, I actually gained. There was suddenly a turning point about 6-8 weeks after the horrible things occurred that, against all odds, I decided to have hope and faith.

I spent months praying and talking to G-d. I worked on myself with no guarantees. I prayed to G-d for the future that I held so deeply in my heart and it is with immense gratitude that I get to say that He gave it to me.

Everything that I've learned and everything that I shared prepared me for what I had been asking for. My old self could have never had the future that I wanted. I had to change and transform to be the vessel for the blessings. I had to let go of my ego and speak to G-d from my soul. I had to let go of fear and rely on my faith. I had to transform the way I looked at G-d, to see Him as merciful instead of vengeful, to see Him as my Helper, Partner and Guiding Light. I looked carefully at the messages He brought to me and made the changes I needed to. I learned to look at others differently. I learned to focus on the good in their hearts. I learned that life only mirrors how we feel and I had to change the way I feel about my life and the people in it in order to make the change happen.

Never in my life have I felt happier with myself than I do now. I am not perfect and I still have a lot to learn, but this journey has taught me the joys of faith. What we need to realize is that once we get the thing that we have been praying for, the opportunity for faith is then lost and over. There is a beauty in knowing what we want is coming. It's the most amazing experience to feel G-d taking care of you, even before it happens. There is an indescribable and beautiful closeness that comes from that trust which leads to the most heartfelt and joy-filled "Thank You."

Afterword

As soon as I had finished writing this book, I was tested yet again. It seemed like everything was coming together in the most perfect way and then it was like the vessel had shattered.

The thing is though, every time a vessel shatters, it is only so an even bigger and better vessel can be built. Remember, the bigger the vessel, the more blessings that can fit into it.

When the most recent test happened, I again immediately noticed that it was a test. However, that also came with a feeling of "Oh my G-d, how could this be happening even after all the work that I've done?" I felt distraught and discouraged and for a moment questioned everything that I wrote about in this book.

I remembered what I learned, though, and I thanked G-d for what I was going through. I told G-d that I wish I could thank Him more sincerely but at the least, I wanted to say "Thank You" in whatever way I could because I know that's what I am supposed to do. I acknowledged that I know everything is for the best, but spent many days wondering if "the best" is dictated *for* me or if "the best" is *up to* me.

As I mentioned earlier, most things that we go through in life are to bring our attention to an underlying belief that needs to be changed. I asked myself many times if what I was going through was a "finite" pre-destined decision or just an inner issue I needed to heal.

While the issue initially surfaced during the previous test, this most recent test showed me there was still indeed more to heal. I decided that whether what I am going through is "pre-destined" or just a mirror of my beliefs, I owe it to myself to at least heal things and find out. After all, no matter what, it will only help me to heal it. Even if what I am going through is indeed something that can be changed, it was then destined that I would go through this because that's a part of my life journey and what I came into this life to learn.

Through all of this, I have also learned to become much more humble. So many times, I prayed and used whatever tools just to get what I wanted. For me "wanting" wasn't about material things, but certain things that I wanted to happen to bring joy and happiness, instead of pain.

All of the tools written about in this book are meant to help bring about that positivity. The positive energy almost always needs to precede the positive things we want coming because that is how we build the vessel for it. I have also found that almost all salvations will come as a surprise. Whenever those magical moments have happened for me, they have always been when I have surrendered, let go or given up. I still had hope, but I had let go of the subject long enough for a positive change to happen. *Miracles always seem to wonderfully catch me off-guard.*

When we focus our attention so strongly on something, it's almost like it can't change. It becomes like a deer in headlights, frozen. Whenever we focus on what isn't going right, it essentially gets stuck in that state, but if we take our attention and thoughts away from it, even for a split second, it's enough time for the issue to change.

So, while I wanted to end this book by telling everyone that I got everything I have been praying for, I am instead writing that I have faith that it will come. You see, for me, this test is about healing an inner belief which I am still in process of. It's also about me becoming my strongest and best self. Every time that I have reached a state of being the most "me," that is when the miracles happen. It's a state of being so centered and strong in myself that I become like my own solar system with the things that I desire in my orbit.

When I am the strongest version of me, I attract what I want and "need" so there is no pain or "chase." I am so blessed to have received this information and even more blessed to be able to share it with you, but the real test now is to practice everything that I've learned and taught to keep myself in that aligned, positive and faith-filled state.

It is with the same information that I have shared with you, that I will continue to do my inner work and get to build another vessel, this time, G-d willing, bigger and strong enough for everything I have been praying for and more.

Remember, we are the vessel that we build.

MY JOURNAL

Much of what I have learned and shared is based on my personal journal. When I initially started journaling, the purpose was to write affirmations and other positive things. I didn't have the intention to share it. I was merely using it as a tool. When certain concepts and things came to me, I felt a strong urge to share certain messages. While I cannot share everything, I am choosing to share the most relevant pages showcasing the progression of my journey and the lessons I've learned.

My first journal pages were written during Chanukah in December of 2018. After lighting the menorah each night, I wrote a page full of affirmations, hoping to bring extra positive energy into my life. My main journaling started the following February.

2/14/19

I am safe. I am loved.

I give permission to let go of control so good things can come easily to me.

I am ready to release guilt.

I am loved, I deserve to be loved and I should never feel like I am a burden or like I am not good enough.

I am good at my job. It's time that I show it. Results count. I am worthy of good things.

I am thankful for all that I have, especially my love and support.

I am ready for my next (safe) emotional release to rid myself of fear and doubt.

I deserve only good things – that is self-love.

GUILT

I have been so hard on myself – it's time to let that go.
I have felt like I am not good enough – it's time to let that go.
Shame has no place in my life.
Guilt has no place in my life.
I am safe.
It is safe to let these emotions go.

I FORGIVE

I forgive myself for being a perfectionist.
I forgive myself for making mistakes.
I forgive myself for being cruel to myself instead of being kind.
I forgive myself for pushing myself too far.
I forgive myself for work mistakes.
I forgive myself for interpersonal mistakes.
I forgive myself for being unkind.
I forgive myself for needing to protect myself.
I forgive myself for feeling like I need to protect myself.
I forgive myself for being demanding.
I forgive myself for needing attention.
I forgive myself for being mad at myself for needing attention.
I forgive myself for being a burden.
I forgive myself for hating myself for being a burden.
I forgive myself and give myself permission to be honest.
I forgive myself and let myself grow.

I am happy that I am taking steps to help myself.

I am healing.

I forgive myself for not eating healthily. I am proud of myself for starting to change that.

This is the beginning of the rest of my life – physically, emotionally, mentally, spiritually.

Good things await me.
I believe the bad things that happened to me are what has inspired me to make change.
I am grateful to G-d.
I am healing. I am safe.
I am going to heal fully.
This is my time to heal.
I am safe.

2/19/19

Guilt vs. Remorse

"I'm sorry" doesn't have to mean "I feel bad".

I am noticing that when I feel guilty about something (like running late or inconveniencing someone), I say the words "I feel bad".

Louise Hay says that physical pain is caused by guilt. I'm wondering if the subconscious mind can tell the difference between physical and emotional pain.

I have been working to release my guilt and in the process, I have become aware of my words. That's what I need to change – how do I respond emotionally and verbally when I would normally feel guilt?

How do I replace the feeling of guilt?

Guilt is different than remorse.
Guilt has negative self-judgment, remorse is an apologetic regret.

I need to not feel bad for needing people, time, space or things.

If I do something I shouldn't (like run late), I can make notes on how to improve myself but I need to learn to just apologize and not feel bad afterwards.

Guilt and pain no longer have a place in my life.

2/19/19

I am strong.
I am beautiful.
I am needed.
I am loved.
I am safe.
I am pleasant.
I am hopeful.
I am happy.
I am healthy.
I am positive.
I am secure.
I am confident.
I am wealthy.
I am smart.
I am kind.
I am creative.
I am respected.
I am cared for and about.
I am independent.
I am my best self.
I have a lot to offer.
My love is reciprocated.
I am appreciated.
All is well.

4/4/19

I AM WORTHY.

I am worthy of being liked.
I am worthy of good things.
I am worthy of being loved.
I am worthy of being appreciated.
I am worthy of feeling good enough.
I am worthy of feeling respected.
I am worthy of positive responses.
I am worthy and deserving of kind words.
I am worthy of forgiveness.
I am worthy of healing.
I am worthy of good treatment.
I am worthy of good outcomes.
I am worthy of healthy relationships.
I am worthy of thoughtfulness.
I am worthy of apologies.
I am worthy of faithfulness.
I am worthy of security.
I am worthy of positive outcomes.
I am worthy of good news.
I am worthy and deserving of all good things.
Good things come easily to me.

4/5/19

I am choosing to let go of control for the things that I cannot control.

I choose to remain hopeful where I should.

My intuition always guides me.

I am safe, I am loved.

Everything happens for a reason and when needed, the "why" is apparent to me.

My emotional growth will lead to good things.

I cannot control time or circumstance, but what's meant to be mine will be. I am therefore choosing to heal. I am Divinely guided and protected. I want to surrender to my Healer. I want to surrender so I can let G-d do G-d's job. I only want to control what I need to and should control. The rest is up to G-d.

I feel safe knowing G-d is taking care of me. I refuse to go back to my old patterns. It's safe to let go of control where I need to.

I trust Divine timing.

I am thankful for Divine guidance.

4/14/19

I safely release my guilt, self-doubt and feelings of unworthiness. I choose to replace these feelings with joy, happiness, love, calmness, clarity, feeling worthy and feeling secure.

If I give myself the love that I need, I no longer have a void. I no longer have a need. All "needy" energy goes away. I allow myself to attract the love and abundance of good things that I deserve. I allow myself to heal physically and emotionally. I safely release all the need for "excuses." (I believe needing excuses caused a lot of the chronic issues I have been dealing with, so I also believe I can eliminate the need for excuses and heal myself.)

I safely replace self-doubt with self-confidence.

There is a beautiful spiritual light that shines from within me. I will succeed. I will triumph. I will become my best self.
Good things are happening for me.
All my positive goals will be met.

4/14/19

I am happy, healthy and wealthy. I am becoming my best self.

I am attracting the good things that I want. I am healing.

Business/career: When I walk into a room for a networking event, I am confident. My energy is that of a successful person. A successful person does not "chase" other successful people; they just go about their business knowing they belong, greeting their peers and enjoying meeting others to network with.

Personal: A person who feels love also doesn't chase. They just embrace.

I choose to love myself unconditionally and embrace myself. I choose to feel comfortable with love. I have everything I need. I am loved.

4/14/19

Words to say to myself in the mirror:

I love you unconditionally.
I feel safe with you.
I feel comfortable with you.
I enjoy your company.
You are my priority.
You make me happy.
I want to spend as much time with you as possible.
I am committed to you.

Affirmations:

I love myself unconditionally.
I accept myself wholeheartedly.
I feel safe and secure.
I am comfortable with myself.

I am my priority.
I create my own happiness.
I am committed to loving myself, healing myself and giving myself the support that I need.

4/16/19

I allow myself to receive money, healing and everything else that I need. I safely eliminate any emotional blocks to my success and reach my goals with the utmost happiness.

I allow all of my "excuses" to go away and for my life to improve. I allow everything to go well in my life so I can keep the emotional energy I need to be successful. I allow my life to be easy. I deserve good things.

I allow good energy and healing to come into my life. Everything is working out for me. I am healing. I am safe. I am loved. I am successful. I have everything that I want and need that's good for me. I allow G-d to surprise me in unexpected ways with the utmost happiness. Everything is working out for me. Everything I prayed for is happening. I am so thankful for my wonderful life. All is well.

4/22/19

G-d gives us everything we need. I think that's why "needy" energy does not attract what we want. When we NEED something, it's almost like a complaint that we don't have it and it's like telling G-d that He didn't already give us everything we need.

We should realize that everything we need, we either have or it is coming to us. Instead of saying we need something, we should ask G-d how to access it.

Everyone has a pipeline/stream of good things. (In Hebrew, we call it Shefa. Abraham Hicks refers to this as the "vortex.") If we don't feel we have what we need currently in our lives, we should realize that it is in our pipeline/stream and may have gotten stuck there. That is why we should ask how to access it.

This randomly came into my head and I felt like I was meant to write it down. I kept wondering how to not feel needy with certain things and now I just got my answer.

4/23/19

A thought came to me this morning that I've had several times before – any time we focus our energy on other people, we take the power away from ourselves.

Think of it this way – do you ever see a marathon runner looking back at others running while racing to the finish line?

Successful people don't compare themselves to others or worry about where other people are. They focus on their mission.

I feel like there is such a lesson in that. As someone who has such a history of worrying about what others are doing, it's a constant reminder to focus on myself.

Once athletes cross the finish line, then they will look. Life is a series of walks and sprints. Some self-growth is rapid and other self-growth can be more slow. Right now, I'm just working on myself, my thoughts and my power. I trust G-d to handle the rest.

4/27/19

I learned a lot over the end of the holiday (Passover) and on Shabbat (the Sabbath). I finished reading both *The Secret to Miraculous Salvations* and *The Power is Within You*.

The Secret to Miraculous Salvations taught me that by thinking about someone's negative traits or behaviors in a positive way, you can actually change them by sending them positive energy.

The Power is Within You taught me that everyone comes into this world to do certain things and when you do things for them (rather than give them guidance), they will just get another challenge where they will have to do the same thing.

I've worked immensely on the controlling behaviors that I've had and now I understand a lot better how to help people.

4/30/19

I was trying to think of the best way to explain Law of Attraction and the concept of resistance. I immediately thought of my exercise bike. The bike has resistance gears. If resistance is up, you push and sweat. When resistance is low, you pedal with ease.

I want my life to have all the good things I want to happen, happen with ease.

I choose the path of least resistance.

4/30/19

I choose the path of least resistance.
I choose the path of ease and happiness.
I allow myself to feel happy.
I allow myself to feel good.
I allow myself to release the resistance.
I allow myself to receive the good.
I allow negative thoughts to go away.
I allow my positive thoughts to win.
I allow the utmost wonderful blessings to happen in my life.
I allow Goodness to Reign.
I allow goodness to rain.
I safely release all tension.
I safely release all worry.
I safely release all fear.
I am safe.

Good things are coming to me.
Good things are happening for me.
There is nothing that G-d can't fix.
I create my positive future.
I create my positive destiny.
With G-d's help, anything is possible.
G-d is with me, I shall not fear.

4/30/19

I realized the other day that in addition to thoughts and feelings (vibrations), there is a lightness and heaviness variation of vibrations. I knew there was heavy and light energy but I didn't realize that the vibrational spectrum is just like color hues in their gradients and variance.

Example 1: Excitement can be light as a feather, knowing something positive is happening, and smiling. Excitement can also be jumping up and down in anticipation.

Example 2: Love can feel light when you feel safe and secure and at ease. Love can also be deep, yearning and have strong attachment.

I feel like lighter energies attract and manifest better. When I finally had (monetary) career success, it felt light as a feather, almost surreal and happened with the utmost ease.

5/2/19

Today the words came to me that I should say "I prefer not to" rather than "I can't".

5/5/19

Yesterday, I was thinking about heavy and light energy and how the same applies to food. The other day, I was focusing on raising my vibration (energy) to feel lighter and my body felt so heavy from what I ate that I felt energetically weighed down. I am realizing that my diet needs to also reflect the energy I want to have and that I should incorporate lighter foods (fruits and vegetables) into my diet for that reason. I often toss them into heavier foods (like spinach into pasta) but I'm thinking it may be a good idea to layer them or eat them side by side rather than all mixed together. That way, I have moments of "eating lightness". So that is now a goal for me.

5/6/19

Over the Sabbath, I was telling my friend and her mother some of the things that I have learned. She (the mother) asked me about advice to help her husband who recently had an injury to his shoulder.

I told her that I focus on the fact that the body knows how to heal itself. I compare it to clay. I was a ceramics major and I was taught that clay has a memory, however you build it, even if you try to later modify it, it will naturally morph or try to morph back to its original state. I believe the body works in a similar way. Abraham Hicks also said that the body knows how to heal itself and that we should focus on allowing it.

Affirm: I allow my body to heal quickly and easily.

5/13/19

I allow the things I desire most to come easily to me.

I remember that I don't have to try so hard for things to come easy. Things come easy to me when I let/allow them.

I allow myself to have the most wonderful, amazing, happy, joyful experiences. I am smiling now thinking about them.

So many wonderful things are happening in my life. My life is so fun and so cool. I have everything I want and need. This emotional journey is so wonderfully amazing and what I have learned about Law of Attraction has forever changed my life for the better. I am so grateful! Thank You, G-d.

5/13/19

Important things I've learned:

1. I don't have to try so hard. It's important to relax and allow.

2. There is no need to go to others for validation; they will generally only mirror me. I saw this when I had concerns as well as when I was happy.

3. If I get a negative thought, I quickly shake it out to not give it any "momentum" as Abraham Hicks calls it. I typically say "Ein Ode Milvado" (there is nothing other than G-d) and I choose to think a better thought.

4. I learned that I should focus on *why* I want something, not just that I want it.

5. Have patience. If I did the right thing (focused on myself, felt the right feelings, thought good thoughts) – it's coming.

6. Gratitude!

5/22/19

There are a few things I have been meaning to write down.

1. I realized that saying, "I don't know how but somehow, with G-d's help (xyz) will happen" is my form of surrendering.

2. I've been often saying, "I don't see any reason why (xyz) can't happen" to remove blocks or to see if I have a block.

3. The concept of a windup toy came to me. It very much illustrates the art of letting go. We wind things up with our desires and then we need to free them afterwards (so they can come to us).

5/27/19

This morning I woke up and I realized that it's not about "forcing" things. It's about declaring what I want, feeling positive emotions and feeling as if I already have it. By nature of doing that, the need to force things goes away.

5/27/19

Life is like a slingshot.

We state our desire (put the ball or stone in).

We build momentum (we pull the bands backwards).

But we have to release and let go to let our desires fly so we can hit our targets.

When we try to control things, it's like never letting go of the slingshot.

6/10/19

I am worthy of good things.
I am deserving of good things.

I choose to attract good things.

I forgive myself for being harsh to myself. I forgive myself for saying unkind words. I forgive myself for thinking negative thoughts and I forgive myself for feeling negative emotions when I know how to do differently.

6/20/19

Yesterday, I wrote in one of my shower notes (a waterproof notepad used in the shower) that one of my biggest areas of progress where I have truly made a positive change is my focus on my own self and independence. I no longer feel the need to rely on anyone else for physical, emotional, mental, spiritual or financial comfort or security.

So much of my past was looking at others and even though I struggled a bit this past month, at least I focused on myself and I am proud of that!

Yesterday, I wrote another note to myself saying that when we look to others for something and get a negative response, we often say "we are worthy" of better. The counter argument is the Higher Self saying "if you are so worthy, why aren't you putting effort into yourself?"

The point is — everything changes from the inside out.

6/20/19

I asked my iPhone what the opposite of the word "doubt" is.

The answers I got were:

Certainty
Confidence
Sureness
Trust
Faith
Solution

I know with **absolute certainty** that everything in my life will continue to get better. I have the **utmost confidence** in myself to be happy, healthy and successful. I know with **absolute sureness** that everything will work out for me.

I **trust** good things are falling into place for me. I have **faith** that everything is working out for me and that I will find many happy **solutions**. Life is good.

6/23/19

I am safe.
I am loved.
I am happy.
I am healthy.
I am joyful.
I am smart.
I am creative.
I am healthy.
I am healed.
I trust in complete faith.
I am taken care of by G-d every moment of my life.
I am secure.
I am confident.
I am self-sufficient.
I am excited.
I feel good.
I experience good things.
I enjoy my life.
I have fun.
All is well.
Everything is working out for me.
Thank You, G-d.

I trust G-d, my Healer.
I trust G-d, my Fixer.
I trust G-d, my Provider.

Thank You, G-d.

7/9/19

My friend, Meira, sent me several YouTube videos of Gedale Fenster, a religious Jewish entrepreneur and motivational speaker. He said that the Shefa (stream of blessings) is always coming down, but we need to be in a place to receive it.

He is talking about the importance of faith. He said at all times, it's either trust or anxiety.

He also spoke about the importance of looking up to G-d, instead of looking down in depression. Any time I've had any intuition, it was when I was looking up. When I have thoughts, I feel like I should check whether my head is up or down when they come into my head. (Not counting when I'm journaling of course, although I do lift my head up a lot while writing.)

He said that the more we look up, the more we get from our Shefa.

He is talking about how even our forefathers had times of doubt and when they did, that's when the negative forces took hold.

I see how I was in such a place of faith, how one (negative) thought led to a month of crying and worry. Thank G-d, I know how to fix it.

G-d, I am so immensely grateful for all You have taught me and shown me. You showed me hope, love and faith. I am so grateful to know that all I have to do is have faith in You. Please G-d, help me on the road to get there. Please help me to be strong in my faith and to trust in You.

EIN ODE MILVADO. (There is nothing other than G-d.)

7/10/19

This is a note that I found in my phone from June 24th:

"If I really had faith, I would allow myself to take time for myself without worry. And, if I really had faith, I'd be able to have an expectation without worry tied to it."

If we hold onto a negative expectation, positivity cannot flow as easily.

We can create goals and expectations. We should acknowledge that with G-d's help, anything is possible and take joy in that. If we are struggling, it's okay to start off with a smaller goal and ask G-d to help us build up our faith.

7/10/19

Things I've learned over the past couple of months:

- All changes start from the inside/Life is a mirror

- To stop going to others for advice and to keep things quiet

- To let go of control

- That when I feel sad or worried all I need to do is find one hope and hold onto it

- That G-d wants to give us blessings and that we can ask for the ultimate mercy and have G-d's ultimate mercy help us

- The power of EIN ODE MILVADO (There is nothing other than G-d)

- Everything is G-d. Miracles happen.

- That the past and present do not matter (because we create our future)

- If we change our feelings to more positive ones, good things will come

7/18/19

(Reflecting on my birthday)

Several days before my birthday, I realized that (seemingly) even stronger than gratitude is appreciation. When feeling appreciation, I realized that **appreciation is love**.

7/24/19

Good things come to me easily.

Money comes to me easily.

It's easy for me to make money.

Money comes to me in unexpected ways.

An abundance of money allows me to feel ease.

I am aligned with money.

I love having money so I can help people.

I love having money to fund my goals.

I love and appreciate money.

7/28/19

While in the shower, I felt the underlying issue to the doubt and self-doubt I have been dealing with – it is the fear of being wrong.

With a certain issue, it was a fear of making a wrong or bad decision – meaning feeling like I couldn't trust myself or my judgment.

Even now as I deal with "am I right or are others right about my life?" I see this going on there.

I hereby safely release my fear of being wrong and all of its negative manifestations in my life.

I hereby choose to live in the joy of the moment, trusting my love, my instincts, and my Higher Self. When G-d created me, He knew the choices I would make and I believe He accounted for them in my destiny.

I know everything will be okay.

Thank You, G-d.

7/28/19

I trust that what I've done is enough.

With my current situation, I have done much self-improvement, worked to change thought patterns and actions and at some point (meaning now), I have to trust that what I've done is enough and I need to let G-d do G-d's job.

Sometimes I get too wrapped up in this "Law of Attraction" thing that I feel like I need to fix everything. G-d gives me all of the answers, thoughts, feelings, and circumstances I need. Now is my time to step back. Now is my time to trust. Now is my time to believe. Now is my time to have faith. Now is my time to know G-d is taking care of me. He has heard my prayers. Thank You, G-d.

8/4/19

On Friday, I prayed and asked G-d to help me pray in a more efficient way. I said something like "G-d, I know you're listening, but how can I pray in a more efficient way?" Within minutes, the words "be strong in your convictions" went running through my veins.

In general, it seems G-d has been showing me that I need to know exactly what I'm saying and what I'm asking and should do so without fear.

8/11/19

I choose to feel good about myself, my life and my future.

Good things come easily and naturally to me.

I have the ability to make everything in my life get better.

It's okay for me to have my desires.

I am loved.

I am safe.

I can trust myself.

I go with the flow of life.

I am Divinely guided and protected.

I see how much I am loved.

Money flows to me easily.

8/11/19

I am human.
I make mistakes.
I forgive.
I am forgiven.
There are things that I need.
There are things that I desire.
I have good days.
I have not as good days.
I deserve to be loved.
I deserve to be respected.
I deserve to be appreciated.
I deserve to be prioritized.
I deserve to feel good.
I deserve to be accepted.
I deserve to feel special.
I deserve to feel worthy.
I deserve the best.
I deserve happiness.

Even if I am not perfect, I deserve good things. We are all human. If I can accept others, they can accept me.

I am not a burden. I am an asset.

Thank You for loving me.

8/18/19

I TRUST MYSELF.

I TRUST G-D.

I TRUST THE PROCESS OF LIFE.

I am loved. I feel G-d's love. I see that G-d is giving me love. I am thankful and appreciative of all the knowledge I have received.

Life should be easy and I hereby declare that I allow it to be!

I know what I want and I allow it to happen without being forced.

8/18/19

I remember Chinese finger traps from when I was a kid — such a metaphor for life.

If you run and worry, if you pull away from G-d and try to take matters into your own hands, if you have fear and don't trust the process of life, then you have the "pull".

If you surrender, give it up to G-d, try to not take everything into your own hands and let yourself be vulnerable, you release all control and resistance — you come close to G-d, salvation happens and you are freed from what trapped you.

The point is, faith is often counter-intuitive to logic. Doing the unlikely, like giving yourself a break when you've been stressed about money and working too hard, can actually lead to sudden success and money. The same is true in one's personal life — come close and give the stress a rest.

8/25/19

I am happy.

I am worthy.

My hard work is paying off.

I am healing.

I feel loved.

I am prioritized.

I am chosen.

I am favorited.

I feel joy.

I feel lightness.

I feel ease.

I feel balanced.

I feel safe.

I feel unconditional, reciprocated love.

I feel validated.

I feel smart.

I feel wise.

I feel cared for.

I feel invited.

I feel openness.

I feel accepted.

I feel wanted.

8/27/19

A lot of the "Law of Attraction," as well as general "success" books and videos, talk about the importance of visualization. Well, I didn't know how to visualize myself as a millionaire or visualize most other strong desires. When it comes to money, I didn't have any major goals of what I wanted to buy, I just like the idea of financial freedom. The real reason why I want to have money is to support my future family.

That being said, this morning I woke up and simply asked myself a question while getting ready for a client appointment: "What would a millionaire wear?" That became "What would I wear if I was a millionaire?" and then that became "What's the closest thing to what I would wear if I was a millionaire that I currently have in my closest?" I got dressed and had a great appointment.

9/9/19

I want to forgive.

I want to be forgiven.

I no longer want to hold anger in my body or in my soul.

Anger no longer serves me a purpose.

I safely release all anger tied to fear.

I choose to let go of control and feel safe.

I am Divinely guided and protected.

I trust Divine timing.

All is well.

I am safe.

Good things come easily.

I allow love.
I allow forgiveness.
I am safe.

I allow love.
I allow forgiveness.
I am safe.
I allow love.
I allow forgiveness.
I am safe.

9/15/19

Last week, I was listening to a lot of Gedale Fenster's videos. He was talking about the importance of being a vessel for G-d's blessings and that if we don't have the proper vessels, then the light/blessings shatter it.

I feel like I finally started to understand this concept. I know G-d wants to give me blessings and is giving me blessings, but I need to be ready for them. I am working on that now.

9/20/19

Everything changes from the inside out. G-d, thank You for reminding me of this, please help me.

Please G-d, assist me in knowing what to do and how to help myself.

Please G-d, in this moment, please show me how to have faith and be positive without taking control.

Thank You, G-d, for bringing this to my attention.

Please G-d, show me how to ready myself for and accept the blessings you are giving me.

Please G-d, help me to forgive and feel safe.

Please G-d, help me to feel Your loving energy.

9/25/19

Yesterday my energy was not in a good place so before bed, I decided to listen to a Gedale Fenster lecture on YouTube.

Again he spoke about the idea of being a vessel in order to receive blessings. He said that blessings are always coming down. He compared it to someone having an umbrella over them at the beach, complaining that they aren't getting any sun. He also gave the analogy of when you water plants, if you give them too much water, they can drown.

When he said that, I realized something. In all of the secular "Law of Attraction" information, it says you have to see it and feel and essentially experience it ahead of time. Now I understand that belief and readiness and a person's own ability to gradually ease into it is what makes the vessel for the light. We mentally and emotionally prepare ourselves for what G-d wanted to give us all along.

9/29/19

This morning when I woke up, the following thought saved me:

G-d would not take me this far just to leave me hanging.

G-d is helping me.

G-d is guiding me.

I believe with complete faith that G-d is answering my prayers and is giving me what I have been praying for.

G-d is giving me miracles.

Thank You, G-d.

10/2/19

Something that I have been thinking about for a few months is the idea of being able to easily change your reality. I visualize a knob, kind of like one from an old TV set and I say or think, "I'm changing my reality to one where...." I have in mind that it is just an improved version of my actual reality and that good things are only a knob-turn (mindset change) away.

10/4/19

G-d is just.

Blessed is my Healer.

Blessed is my Fixer.

Blessed is He who is compassionate and understanding.

Blessed is He who has answered my prayers.

Blessed is He who gives me good even if I have doubted the circumstance.

Blessed is He who gives me good even when I lost faith.

Blessed is He who surprises me with wonderful things.

Blessed is He who shows me goodness, gladness, truth, love and happiness.

Blessed is G-d, my compassionate King.

10/15/19

I've been thinking about the importance of decision-making.

In the past, I struggled a lot with decision-making but as I read books like *Think and Grow Rich*, I keep hearing how that is part of success. I often now relate decision-making to using a GPS. A person can always make another decision and change directions. Therefore, I allow myself to make decisions.

The thing is, I realized that once I make a decision, I need to allow G-d to fill in the details. My "GPS coordinates" don't have to be "realistic." My decision should be based on desires and what feels right to me. I use faith and trust to guide me on my journey.

10/24/19

Today, I am choosing to feel good.

I have the power to feel good.

I have the power to get myself back on track.

I have the power to change my life in the most positive way.

Good things come to me easily.

I allow good things to come to me easily.

I know G-d is giving me blessings and I choose to accept and focus on them.

Miracles are always happening for me.

Miracles also happen for those who I care for.

Today is a good day.

I choose to feel good.

11/3/19

Some things that have been helping me a lot lately:

- When I get a negative thought, I tell myself "that's just a stupid thought" or that it was based on my old way of thinking.

- Saying "Thank You" to G-d (randomly) over and over again. I also say EIN ODE MILVADO (There is nothing other than G-d.)

- I pray for help to get my energy right. Sometimes before this, I will say something like "I have the power to make my energy better."

11/3/19

I am loved.

I am chosen.

I am accepted.

I am prioritized.

I am remembered.

I am fun.

I am safe.

I am appreciated.

I am preferred.

My company is enjoyed.

The right opportunities come easily to me.

Those I love make time for me.

Life is always getting better.

Sometimes I get wonderful surprises.

It's easy for me to see the good in others.

I am beautiful.

Those I care for see how special I am.

I am respected.

I am cared for.

I am my priority and the priority of those who love me.

Life is for me.

I always get the love I need.

11/3/19

I have the power to visualize what I need.

I have been feeling emotional the last several days. Because I was feeling down, I took a moment to speak to G-d and tell Him what I feel I need. I told Him that I am so thankful for what I have, but unfortunately have been in a place of worry. When asking for what I feel I need, I was reminded that I have power to visualize what I need.

When we visualize positive images and allow ourselves to feel that energy, we then bring that goodness to ourselves.

11/5/19

Earlier today, I cried and looked in the mirror. I told myself that I loved myself and chose to accept that I was in a state of worrying rather than battling it. At that moment, I surrendered and felt much better.

Generally, I've learned how to get myself into better moods, but today, I did the best thing I could and I accepted where I was at. I forgave myself and stopped being hard on myself for not being able to make myself feel better.

Right after that, something happened that made me smile.

11/7/19

Today is a new day.
This moment is a new moment.
I choose to be positive.
I know there is good in every situation.
I choose to see the good in every situation.
I choose to feel good.
I choose to allow good things to come to me.
I choose to forgive.
I choose to be happy and free of worry.
I am safe. I am loved. All is well.

One of the biggest lessons I've learned is not to try too hard. One of the greatest realizations I've just had is that worry comes in when I think about where I am and where I want to be and I try to control the pathway to get there.

The pathway is up to G-d.

G-d fills in the details. G-d does everything for me, so all I need to do is relax and be thankful in the moment.

11/8/19

Today, I woke up in a funk, but then a positive shift happened. I remembered how I prayed on Rosh Hashana (the Jewish New Year) and cried tears of joy. I told G-d that I know how powerful it was for me to say "Thank You" and that I knew I was meant to have an amazingly wonderful year. The moment I focused on the fact that G-d wants good for me and that good is coming, my entire energy shifted. I no longer worried about the "pathway" of what is happening now, but the fact that good is coming. I know from past experiences and from all that I've learned, just how powerful that positive energy is. When a person is in a place of trust and faith and doesn't worry about the present, good has to come. Positive energy attracts positive energy. I found myself focusing on the "how" (control) instead of the "what" (faith and trust that what I want is coming). When I shift my thoughts, it allows me to have a great day. I told myself over and over again this morning out loud that today is going to be a great day. I told G-d that I know because of the way that I prayed that good has to come. I know how special those tears of "Thank You" are, but more importantly, I know G-d wants to give me good.

Today is going to be a great day.
I allow today to be a wonderful, happy, awesome day.
I allow good things and good news to flow easily to me.
I allow money to come easily to me.
I allow all interpersonal relationships to be harmonious.
I allow great and fun business opportunities to present themselves.
I allow myself to feel loved and grateful.
I allow positive reassurance.
I allow positive personal growth and change.
I allow myself to be at ease and have a great day.

11/8/19

I find it very fun to change my vibration (energy) to that of being in a fun vibration because then life has to cooperate.

I've used that energy in the past with a couple of people in business that I had issues with and it worked amazingly well. Suddenly, people were friendly and happy to see me. For that reason, today I am choosing to be in the vibration of fun.

Today is going to be a great day.

11/20/19

Today, I am choosing to shift my inner worry (block) of "is what I want ever going to happen?" to the (open vessel of) "I'm letting go of control and letting G-d handle things."

I'm really proud of myself for getting to this point.

I'm eager and excited for the amazing experiences to come my way.

When things turned backwards, I kept saying that a negative precedes a positive so I know good is coming.

I am safely releasing all controlling (micromanaging) energies to allow G-d to do G-d's work. I know something (or many amazing things) will come from this. Thank You, G-d.

11/23/19

Over the Sabbath, a really important realization came to me — many actually. There was a certain feeling that I was trying to heal, the one that kept attracting (feelings of) loneliness. At first I thought it was "worthiness," then I thought it was being a "priority"/"prioritized," but I couldn't quite get the exact word/feeling/emotion. The thing is feeling "wanted".

Since my childhood, I felt unwanted and cast out. I had identified much of where it came from, but not sure yet if I found the root cause. The thing is, I want people to want to spend time with me, who see my value and prioritize me.

I safely release my feelings of being unwanted and I allow myself to be loved.

12/10/19

This is what came to me last night:

Life always mirrors where we are at. I knew everything I learned about Law of Attraction would come in handy with this challenge but I thought the challenge was to get myself to feel better/get into a better vibration because when you feel good, good things happen. I thought it was just a challenge to change my energy. I knew it was such a powerful thing when I believe that G-d's Power is above all else, but I had trouble really connecting to that emotion of having faith and feeling good. Now I realize it's because I needed to see that the inner belief I held was what was causing the pain. I thought it was feelings of worthiness of being good enough or "not being chosen" – it's closest to the last one (as I wrote about in my previous journal entry). My deep inner belief was never healed. So even though I believe G-d's Power is above all else and even though I managed to be positive, G-d had to have me fall emotionally so I could realize the belief that caused it. Now, I can heal.

Thank You, G-d.

12/15/19

EIN ODE MILVADO (the concept that there is nothing other than G-d) and "Law of Attraction" are in essence, the same thing.

Ein Ode Milvado is the concept that everything is G-d.

Law of Attraction is an amazing awareness and alignment tool.

The past several days, really all of last week, I felt incredibly powerful as I felt aligned and connected to G-d. I felt weird about how "powerful" I felt (like I could accomplish/do anything with G-d's help) but I realized it's a normal feeling to feel powerful since I am aligning with the most Powerful Source there is — G-d.

G-d is in every person, every situation — everything. He uses our outer world to reflect to us what we need to work on/rectify/fix.

Therefore, all Law of Attraction is, is cleverly marketed "Ein Ode Milvado."

12/20/19

This week my energy shifted from a "needy energy" to "I know I am needed."

It's a powerful change personally and professionally.

Thank You, G-d.

I provide value.

I know I am valuable.

I feel my worth.

Thank You, G-d for Your abundant blessings. Thank You for answering my prayers.

12/31/19

I do not have the power to change someone else. I have the power to work on me and that is where my power lies. My power is in the present moment and I choose to improve it. While I cannot (directly) change others, I can use my voice and take inspired action to make change. G-d decides whether I am successful or not. Those I speak to can choose to listen to my words. I think creating awareness is helpful and it's okay to want to make change but the results are up to G-d.

Thank You, G-d.

12/31/19

2020 is the (secular) year of me going from *wanting* to *having*.
(I celebrate both the secular and Jewish New Year. The Jewish New Year is Rosh Hashana.)

Please G-d, may it be Your will to fill my positive desires.

12/31/19

My goal for 2020 is to shift from being in a place of "wanting" to a place of "having".

I looked through my first journal and it was heavy with my "wants". While it's good that I have my desires, keeping them in a place of "wanting" makes it somewhat out of reach. That is why I am working on shifting my perspective from being in a state of "wanting" to the things I desire being on their way to me.

My goal is to continue to better myself, to let go of control as best as I can, to no longer "micro-manage" my prayers and to let G-d do His job.

I have no doubt that 2020 will be the best year of my life so far.

I am grateful for all that I learned in 2019.

1/7/20

In dealing with certain personal issues, I had realized instead of looking to others, that I should be my own favorite person.

I realized that I should be my own favorite person. I do love myself, but now I see how important it is to love myself the most.

- I choose to love myself more than anyone else.
- I am my own favorite person.

When I previously journaled about not feeling prioritized or preferred, I thought about the mirror concept. *How could I be someone else's favorite person if I'm not my own?*

1/7/20

Earlier today when I prayed (even before what I wrote earlier), it helped me put my focus back on me.

I asked G-d to help me make the changes I need to make within myself in order to have what I most desire.

Everything changes from the inside out.

1/9/20

Today, I thought about myself in relation to what I want and where I want to be. I was reminded that if I'm not there, that all I need to do is "shift" (gradually move) into that version of me. It's always helpful to ask myself what the version of me will be like when the thing I desire is happening. For example: What habits will I have or not have? What setting am I in? Etc.

Also, I realized that a good way to explain "shifting" is similar to something I've seen when watching football. Often, when a player catches the ball but knows he can only go so far with it, he will start to spin in circles (so no one can grab him) and then push himself a tiny bit just to make it over the next closest yard line.

I feel like life is like that because we can't always run to where we want but we can always inch closer.

1/14/20

In speaking with my mom, I told her from a place of sadness that I felt like with the test I was experiencing, it was sort of like I wasn't in my normal reality. Meaning, life was going well and then it went backwards as life sometimes does. What I was experiencing felt odd, almost false because I felt like I should be in a better place. After saying multiple times that this didn't feel like "my reality," I realized I could use the same concept to describe the reality I want and am familiar with. I then started to affirm my way into it. Remember, our reality is created by our perception, so when I am talking about changing my reality, I am really talking about changing my perception.

In my reality, I know everything I've gone through supports where I want to be.
In my reality, I am starting to feel more positive and starting to feel relief.
In my reality, I know anything is possible.
In my reality, I overcome my fears.
In my reality, I know I am safe on my journey.
In my reality, things are changing for the better and are in line with my desires.
In my reality, I feel good-feeling thoughts.
In my reality, I am becoming my best self.

I choose to center myself.
I choose to feel good.
I choose to be my positive self.
I choose to love myself.

As I become my best self and I connect with who I am, my life rapidly and drastically changes for the better. I see immediate reflection of me changing myself for the better.

1/14/20

I AM...

A strong spiritual force within a beautiful human body

A hopeful, positive, eager and excited, happy person

Someone who attracts amazing opportunities and the love and communication I desire

Someone who overcame anxiety and negative predictions who believes anything is possible

Strong in my love and strong in my views

Forgiving, understanding and someone who knows the future is different from the past when it comes to peoples' positive evolution and change

I love and forgive unconditionally.

1/14/20

The true me is understanding, loving and forgiving.

The true me knows that what feels right and joyous to me feels that way for a positive reason.

The real me is so strong in who I am that I attract the good things that I want.

I see which beliefs pull me towards and away from who I truly am.

I choose to focus on the positive beliefs that support who I am.

Through my centering and self-love, I attract the positive reality which I desire because after all, I desire it for a reason.

1/17/20

I'm realizing that "not chasing" is part of the self-love thing.
It falls into my theory of needing to be my own Universe and attract positive things to me by feeling good about myself.

Dr. Jacquilen Tomas, Ali, the holistic practitioner who introduced me to the concept of self-love, helped me to begin this journey. All of my journaling and all of my going back and forth led me right back to where I started. I ended my book saying that I owe it to myself to get back on track and to finish the process I started. In order to do that, I had to utilize the information that I learned and wrote about in this book. I also began reciting again the initial self-love affirmation that she gave me, in addition to my daily prayers. What happened throughout the story I shared is that I veered off track from fear. A long time ago Jacquilen told me something that I didn't understand until recently and that was that fear and love can't hold the same place. I'm starting to understand now what that means.

I have reminded myself that life mirrors where we are at, so my decision to heal myself comes from a place of self-love. My decision to keep pursuing what's important to me also comes from a place of self-love. My ability to forgive and be understanding also comes from a place of self-love because the person I am is a loving and forgiving person.

Every time I have been my happiest is when I have loved myself and had a strong sense of self. The times where I felt like I "had the most" was when I was strong within myself, when I was content within myself, when I relied on myself and when I put my energy on myself (instead of others). When I focused on what others around me were doing, I took that power away from myself because as I keep stating, all power lies within. I know when I focus on myself everything falls into place because anything "out of place" was only to show me what I needed to work on and that my attention should only be on me.

POINTS TO REMEMBER

- Focus on what you desire, not what you lack.

- Our words create our reality, be extremely careful with how you speak about yourself and others and in general with what words you choose to use.

- Saying daily affirmations can help you to quickly and easily get to your goals.

- Never chase anything, especially love, money or attention. Instead focus on loving yourself and seeing your value, then what you want will come to you.

- The point of visualization and similar tools is to get you to feel comfortable with the subject matter so it is no longer on a pedestal and therefore attainable. It also helps the subconscious mind.

- Whatever your current situation is, it is something that you created from your past thinking and past self. There is so much power in the present moment and you can start to create a better future for yourself. Meaning, whatever you're experiencing now is only temporary.

- Our emotions should be *proactive*, not reactive.

- Ask yourself "what is the dominate vibration (energy) that I am emitting?" (fear, anger, excitement, happiness, love)

- Noticing your energy is incredibly helpful. Once identified, you can help yourself change your vibration.

- When you pray, try not to beg for whatever it is that you need help with. Do your best to humbly pray with confidence and faith that your prayers are being answered. Feel good about what you are accomplishing by praying.

- Remember to practice gratitude.

- Every morning when you wake up say "Thank You" and after that, declare what it is that you want for yourself for the day. Example: "I choose for today to be a great day, a healthy day, a prosperous day, a day where I'm feeling good and feeling positive energy and on track for my goals."

- Knowing what it is that you desire is about 80% of the battle. Be clear on what you want but be OPEN to the pathway to it and trust that it can happen.

- Remember to look for patterns within your life as to what underlying issues you may need to heal.

- Happily accept that growth and positive change are a part of the process. When you shift into a better version of yourself, you become closer and closer to the things you desire.

- Even if you think that the current version of you can never have what you truly desire, know that a version of you can. It's about taking steps to become that version of you.

- Trust yourself and trust the process.

A NOTE ABOUT GRATITUDE

The key to consistent positivity is gratitude.

Gratitude is also what helps us align with and manifest our desires.

When people are truly grateful for what they already have or even if they are just thankful for their personal journey, it puts them in a place energetically of already "having". The energy of having gratitude creates more things to be grateful for.

Gratitude is also what keeps things in a neutral or positive place so the things we desire are not put on a pedestal. Even if we desire something, it won't become the dangerous "I'll be happy when...." When we are happy with our lot, we can then ask for the things we desire without being in a state of "wanting," or worse, complaining.

Also, when we are in a true state of gratitude, there is no fear.

When we are happy with what we have and happy with our circumstances (which we know are there to help us), we can then be happier and more appreciative of our journey.

Also, typically, the more we feel and express gratitude, the more we will be given understanding. The more understanding we have about ourselves and our journey, the easier it is to be grateful.

I know some days it's not easy to find gratitude. When trying to get yourself to feel gratitude, you can make a list of several things you are grateful for, you can try to look at the good in your situation or something that has helped me many times is to just say "Thank You," even if I have no idea why. Sometimes rougher days make us appreciate our really good days and without contrast, maybe we wouldn't appreciate all the good that happens in our lives. Keep in mind though, without tests, we may not grow and everything we go through is with love. We were never meant to be spiritually or emotionally sedentary. Our journeys are each unique and we all have the ability to make our lives better. When you start to truly realize what's happening in your life, you'll see that it's not happening *to* you, it's happening *for* you and that is something to be grateful for.

CONCLUSION

There are people who use Law of Attraction simply to attract what they want. There are people who have abandoned their religious belief systems and instead have adopted this Universal practice as one. From everything that I've learned, I can tell you that Law of Attraction was created to support us and help us in our journey; Law of Attraction in of itself is *not* the journey. Law of Attraction is a tool to help us to better ourselves and come closer to G-d.

To practice Law of Attraction without belief in G-d, or a Higher Power of some kind makes no sense, to quit practicing religion because you "found a way to get what you want" makes no sense. Each person was born into a certain religion and set of circumstances for a reason (even if it changes). We each come into this world to rectify certain things within ourselves and to better the world as a whole. We came into this world to connect with ourselves and our Creator. We came into this world to realize how amazing life is and the journey that comes with it. We came into this world to grow and GIVE THANKS. For whatever we believe, there is one thing more important than everything else and that is *gratitude*. Whatever we are going through, whether it is good or seemingly bad, it is so important to turn to G-d and say "Thank You" because in truth, all situations are opportunities. (*Everything we go through is for the best because it makes us our best!*)

It is my true hope that after reading this book, whether you were already familiar with Law of Attraction or not, that this information helps you put your life into perspective. I hope this information brings you lots of hope, joy, miraculous salvations and closeness to G-d.

Together, may we thank G-d for this life, this journey, this opportunity, this knowledge, this faith and the ability to recognize Him and all He has created.

Thank You

NOTES

(Feel free to use this page to write down any thoughts and ideas that come to you while reading this book.)

Made in the USA
Middletown, DE
03 October 2021